CONCORDIA UNIVERSITY

DU20.L72
PACIFIC HO

W9-AMY-519

3 4211 000026079

130°

Vancouver

California

W

N

40°

30°

vich ls.

vai

Mexico

20°

WITHDRAWN

Galapagos
ls

0°

Peru

Lima

Callao

10°

Marquesas. ls.

w or. Tuamotu.

hiti

Arch

Pitcairn

Easter. ls.

J.Fernandez

20°

Chile

Patagonia

30°

alis

Pt.Desire

40°

ncognita

50°

Magellan. St.

Falkland.ls

Staten.ls

C. Horn

130°

100°

PACIFIC
HORIZONS

by Christopher Lloyd

CAPTAIN MARRYAT
AND THE OLD NAVY

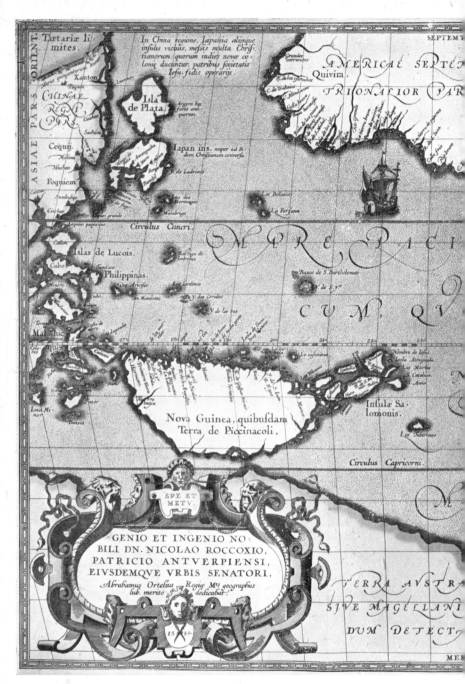

THE PACIFIC IN 1589

Ortelius, *Theatrum Orbis Terrarum*, 1589 ed.

PACIFIC HORIZONS

The Exploration of the Pacific before Captain Cook

by

CHRISTOPHER LLOYD

M.A., F.R.G.S.

Author of *Captain Marryat and the Old Navy*, etc.

for my purpose holds
To sail beyond the sunset, and the baths
Of all the western stars, until I die.
It may be that the gulfs will wash us down;
It may be we shall touch the Happy Isles.

TENNYSON: *Ulysses.*

KLINCK MEMORIAL LIBRARY
Concordia Teachers College
River Forest, Illinois

London

George Allen and Unwin Ltd.

Printed in Great Britain
in 12D point *Walbaum* type
by T. and A. Constable Ltd., Edinburgh.

THE PAPER AND BINDING OF THIS BOOK
CONFORM TO THE AUTHORISED ECONOMY
STANDARD

First published in 1946
All rights reserved

2 0 2 91

PREFACE

THE sound of bombs falling in the Pacific must have aroused the curiosity of many people with regard to the early history of that great ocean. Most of us know something of the achievements of Captain Cook; but what happened before him? What is King Solomon doing in the South Sea? What sort of men found and named islands like Austrialia del Espiritu Santo and L'Enfant Perdu? Who were Juan Fernandez or Bougainville or Wallis?

Cook's name has obscured that of his predecessors. This book tells the story of the exploration of the Pacific before him, from the day when the first European had sight of the South Sea from a peak in Darien to that when, in all essentials, it was mapped and charted by the most painstaking navigator the world has ever known. It was the men of that period, most of them obscure in their own day and forgotten in ours, some, like Drake and Anson, famous for other reasons than for geographical exploration, who set the problem which Cook solved with triumphant finality. If they had not suffered and guessed and talked and narrowed down the limits between which fruitful discoveries might be made, Cook's task would have been beyond even his capacity.

Of all their dreams the most lasting was that of a great southern continent, *Terra Australis Incognita*. Look upon those beautiful maps of the sixteenth and seventeenth centuries and see with what certainty the confines of this legendary land are marked. Even in Cook's day the fading vision was bright enough to make that his first object of discovery. Such myths are always sources of inspiration, but never was there a more fruitful one than this. In a sense, the subject of the following pages is how *Terra Australis Incognita* was reduced to the limits of Antarctica.

Besides telling of such half-forgotten heroes as Mendaña, Quiros, Le Maire, Byron's grandfather, Carteret, M. de Bougainville, I have had another aim in writing this book. Exploration is a co-operative and international task. It is a mistake to look at any enterprise solely from the point of view of one successful man, be he a Cook or a Columbus. Scholars and cartographers and patrons play their part as well as seamen, and the representatives of every nation help to diminish the bounds of the unknown. Every voyage adds something to the map; each nation and each age learns something from its neighbours and its predecessors. That is the chief excuse for historical and comparative studies. The search begun by a Drake or a Quiros in the sixteenth century is still being pursued in the eighteenth, and were it not for nationalistic jealousies and ignorance of what had been done by other men at other times, the paths of the later explorers would have been made easier.

At the same time, every scrap of knowledge brought home widened the intellectual horizon of Europe. Exploration itself is of no account, unless it be as an example of heroism; the way in which the knowledge of the globe and its potentialities is digested, the way in which travellers' tales fertilise the imagination of statesmen and writers at home, that is an aspect of the subject too often omitted. As the learned Harris remarks in his *Navigantium atque itinerarium bibliotheca* (2 vols. folio. 1705): "It is a very happy Circumstance in this kind of Reading, that it charms us by a perpetual Variety, and keeps alive that Thirst of Inquiry, which we are apt to lose, when too closely confined to severer studies." The lure of the South Seas from Defoe to Stevenson, the charm of the savage as imagined by a Rousseau or a Gauguin, is therefore just as much the subject of this book as the heroic enterprises of the idealists, the missionaries, the scientists and the buccaneers who sailed those seas.

As the sense of space is eliminated in the modern world and a depressing uniformity extends its sway over the globe, so that one may wear the same clothes and see the same films in Piccadilly as in Puka Puka, it is well to be reminded of those to whom distance was a reality, who, without adequate charts or instruments, without proper food or medicine, sailed their crazy ships like Ulysses, the prototype of such wanderers, "beyond the sunset." How far they sailed, or where exactly they were, they had no means of telling; but they were convinced that if they pressed on farther on a westerly course they would find something, be it gold, spices, Cathay, or the unknown continent.

> It may be that the gulfs will wash us down;
> It may be we shall touch the Happy Isles.

In the end the survivors usually sailed round the world; the others perished from hunger or shipwreck. The Argument of the *Rime of the Ancient Mariner* is the story of this book: "How a Ship having passed the Line was driven by Storm to the cold Country towards the South Pole; and how from thence she made her course to the tropical Latitude of the Great Pacific Ocean; and of the strange things that befell; and in what manner the Ancyent Marinere came back to his own Country."

I am indebted to the authorities of the Public Record Office and the British Museum, and to Instr. Cmdr. C. W. Baldwin, R.N., for their assistance ; and to Squadron-Leader W. A. Foster for permission to reproduce part of the Blaeu map in his possession.

CONTENTS

LIST OF ILLUSTRATIONS

I

INTO THE SILENT SEA

THE first European to see the Pacific Ocean was Vasco Nuñez de Balboa. On September 25, 1513, the Indian who had guided his party across the isthmus of Darien showed him, from the top of a mountain, the prospect of the southern sea glittering beyond the forests below. Two days later Balboa ran down the beach and plunged waist high into the surf, waving a sword in one hand and a standard in the other, to claim the discovery of an unknown sea in the name of his master, the King of Spain.

Sixty years later Francis Drake had a similar experience, when his Cimaroon guide took him up to a "bower" built in a tree to show him what the Spaniards now called the Mar del Sur. When he had seen it he knelt and "besought Almighty God of his goodness to give him life and leave to sail once in an English ship in that sea." Drake's was the first English ship to sail across the ocean, but another Englishman had crossed it many years before him in the service of Spain, only to perish on the farther shore from the privations he had endured. For with Magellan there had sailed a gunner, "Master Andrew of Bristol," whose bones lie somewhere in the Ladrones or Mariana islands.

Of all voyagers, ancient and modern, Magellan must be deemed the most courageous. He was, wrote a companion, "most versed in nautical charts, and he knew better than anyone the true art of navigation." But what did these charts, this art of navigation amount to? To measure the intrepidity with which Magellan and his like launched out into unknown seas, it is necessary to appreciate not only the poverty of that art, but the strength of the superstitions which clouded the minds of their men. The ancient and terrifying theory of the zones—the frigid, where men froze, and the torrid, where they burned—had indeed been exploded by the Portuguese voyages round the Cape of Good Hope, but that was only a score of years previous to Magellan's voyage, and a popular superstition is not so speedily killed in the minds of sailors. *Frigor inhabitabilis* still marked the northern and southern regions of the charts they knew. *Perusta*, or the burning zone, lay like a belt of fire across the centre, where flames sprang up to lick the sky. *Oceanus quem nemo vidit hominum propter zonam torridam*—that was the boiling sea which had to be traversed in order to sail south of the equator. *Brumae, Mare Tenebrosum*, floating weed which engulfed ships, bat-winged demons with human faces, the Kraken, the octopus which swallowed elephants, the great sea serpent. . . . And if one did surmount these terrors of the deep one might be carried to the Antipodes, where lived the Troglodytes, the Anthropophagi, the Garamantes, and the scaly dragon.

When men first crossed the Pacific the time was not long past when many believed that the earth was shaped like a plate, over the edge of which it was only too easy to sail. Some thought it was pear-shaped, though anybody with any pretensions to learning knew that it was spherical, but not even the most learned clerk could say what was on it. Ptolemy's atlas, revived in the fifteenth century renaissance, was an improvement on those monkish geographers who followed the advice of the blessed Ambrose that "to consider the nature and the position of the earth does not help us in our hopes of the life to come." But Vasco da Gama had shown how inaccurate even it might be when he exploded Ptolemy's conception of the Indian Ocean as a vast inland sea; and to the west Ptolemy marked nothing at all. When Magellan's crew murmured despondently in the mazes of his new strait, he assured them that he was certain of an outlet into the sea beyond, "because he had seen it by a marine chart made by the great pilot and mariner Martin of Bohemia." Apparently he was referring to what we call Behaim's globe, which, since it was constructed before the news of the discovery of America reached Europe, shows nothing of the New World. Only the mythical western islands, beloved of old poets—St. Brendan and the Fortunate Isles—

can be found upon it. The strait is indeed vaguely marked on
Schöner's globe of 1515, on the grounds of a supposed Portuguese
voyage to the westward. Magellan, however, never mentions
such a voyage, and no proof of it has ever been forthcoming.
At least by this date another great sea had been added in the
minds of men to the old conception of the Western and Eastern
oceans. It was becoming increasingly clear, mainly as a result
of voyages to the east, that some great sea stretched beyond the
Spice Islands and Cathay, separating Asia from what was beginning to be called America, but as yet that ocean lacked all
definition, even that of a name.

Equally unreliable were the navigational instruments then
in use, nor did they show any marked improvement for at least
two centuries. The men who first crossed the Pacific Ocean had
no sextants, no chronometers, no nautical almanacs or even
accurate tables. They had to feel their way into the unknown.
Such seamen could rightfully claim as their own the royal
motto of Spain—*Plus Ultra*, further yet! For their latitude
they depended on sights taken with an astrolabe, an instrument
but little changed since Chaucer described it for his son, "litel
Lowis"; in the course of the century the cross staff and back staff
came into use, so that fairly accurate sights could be taken. As
for longitude, no one worried about that. Towards the end of
the sixteenth century a writer complains "there be some that
are very inquisitive to have a way to get the longitude, but that
is too tedious for seamen, since it requireth the deep knowledge
of astronomy, wherefore I would not have any man think that
the longitude is to be found at sea by any instrument; so let no
seamen trouble themselves with any such rule, but (according
to their accustomed manner) let them keep a perfect account
and reckoning of the way of their ship." To obtain this, their
Dead Reckoning, they relied on the three L's—the Log, to
estimate the distance travelled, and the Lead and the Look-out
to steer clear of reefs and shoals. The Log was originally a piece
of wood; later it became a triangular wooden kite standing
upright in the water, and attached to a line marked at regular
intervals with knots of pieces of ribbon. This contraption was

hove overboard every hour, and the speed at which the knots passed across a mark on the deck was measured by an officer standing by with a sandglass in his hand. Hence a "knot" is a measure of the speed at which a ship passes through the water, and to "write up the log" means to chalk up the result on a slate. By such means they attempted to deduce the distance travelled; but as a ship under sail seldom travels at a regular speed on account of the variability of winds and currents, enormous errors were frequent. One of Magellan's pilots is credited with an error of some 3000 miles in his calculations after crossing the Pacific. As late as the middle of the eighteenth century a naval officer under Anson's command could find himself off the east coast of South America when he thought he was off the west.

As for the ships themselves, they were of course mere cockle-shells by modern standards. They must have been wonderfully seaworthy vessels to have achieved the voyages they did, but what strikes one most in the few pictures of them which have survived is their breadth of beam and their high free-board. Their towering poops must have made them very unmanageable with the wind abeam. Furthermore, with the limited sailing gear then in use they could not have sailed at all close to the wind, and they were therefore at the mercy of winds and currents. Hence the route of nearly all the early voyagers across the Pacific is much the same. They had to rely on the Trades to carry them across the ocean from the American coast, and voyages in the contrary direction were out of the question until the wind system of the new ocean began to be known. On a long voyage there was not only the difficulty of waiting for a fair wind to be surmounted; one had also to take into account the depredations of the *teredo navalis*, or naval worm. Every few weeks the ship had to be hauled up on some beach or creek to be careened and patched. At the best of times there was always a foot or two of foul water swilling in the well, the smell of which, mingled with the odour of decaying provisions and foetid water casks, must have turned the strongest stomachs.

Inadequate navigational instruments, no provisions which

ould be preserved, crank ships, clumsy sailing gear and a
mutinous crew—such was Magellan's equipment. But at the
same time he had no fear. In defiance of ignorance and superstition he set sail in 1519 in five "very old and patched ships,"
in which the Portuguese ambassador said he would not adventure
as far as the Canaries. As for the geographer who, together
with an Antwerp spice merchant, backed the enterprise, "I do
not count him for much, for he is half crazy."

Of course the ambassador was prejudiced. Magellan was by
birth a Portuguese, with a limp from a wound received while
fighting for the King of Portugal. At the age of thirty he came
back from the east, quarrelled with the king for refusing to raise
his pension half a ducat, and enlisted in the service of the King
of Spain in order to discover a new route to the Spice Islands via
America instead of Africa. Most probably the real reason for his
voyage was the same as that avowed by the Italian, Antonio
Pigafetta, who sailed with him and kept a valuable journal: that
he was "desirous of seeing the wonderful things of the ocean."

The pattern of Magellan's voyage was to be repeated in
broad outlines by most of the circumnavigators before Cook.
Only one of his five ships returned home; that was to be a
common occurrence, since ships not commanded by skilful,
resolute men were apt to be wrecked or turn back at the entrance
to the South Seas. At St. Julian on the coast of Patagonia he
discovered the last port at which it was possible to careen and
bream before the second and most hazardous part of the voyage
began. Here he had to quell a mutiny. Drake had to do the
same thing at the same spot sixty years later, because it was
here, after a long Atlantic voyage, that the prospect of continuing on a still longer voyage through unknown seas struck the
timorous-hearted with intolerable dismay. Here Pigafetta discovered the Patagonian Giant, "so tall that the tallest of us only
came up to his waist." He was intrigued by their habit of
pushing an arrow two feet down their throats to act as an emetic,
a drastic remedy necessitated by a diet of rats eaten whole and
unskinned. The existence of this monstrous race continued to
exercise the minds of explorers for centuries to come, until more

B

scientific investigators examined them with greater care. Pata
gones—"men with big feet"—Magellan called them, on accoun
of their *guanaco* sandals stuffed with straw, which is the mos
likely explanation of the persistent story of their grea
height.

In his passage through the Straits Magellan was more for
tunate than many of his successors; it took him thirty-eigh
days, compared with the eighty it took several of the eighteenth
century captains. It was he who gave the name of Cape Virgin
to the cape marking the entrance, because he sighted it on the
day of the Eleven Thousand Virgins. His name for the land to
the south, Tierra del Fuego, from the fires he sighted on the
shore, has also remained along with many others. But it is a
pity that his name for the cape marking the Pacific entrance
has been dropped in favour of Cape Pillar, for the change rob
the narrative of its joyous climax: "They (the advance party
told us that they had found the cape and the sea great and wide
At the joy of which the captain general had at this he began to
weep, and he gave the name Cape Deseado to this cape, as a
thing which had been much desired for a long time." "
think," adds Pigafetta, intoxicated with the excitement of the
first that ever burst into that silent sea, "that there is not in the
world a more beautiful country, or a better strait than this one
. . . the sea was well named Pacific (*la mer paisible*)."

His route across was much the same as that followed by other
early circumnavigators, largely because, as we have seen, the
ships of those days were at the mercy of natural forces. Issuing
from the straits at the end of November more by chance than
by calculation, he did not encounter the Westerlies at their
worst. The Peru, or Humboldt, Current swept him north to
an undetermined latitude, probably somewhere near the tropic
where the South-East Trades carried him across the waste o
ocean. By ill chance his course just missed the earthly paradise
which so refreshed his successors, where

Slides the bird o'er lustrous woodland, droops the trailer from the crag,
Droops the heavy-blossomed bower, hangs the heavy-fruited tree—
Summer isles of Eden lying in dark-purple spheres of sea.

or ninety-eight days they sailed without opportunity to pro-
vision the ship, such a voyage "that no man will ever undertake
again." "We ate only old biscuit, brought to powder and
stinking from the dirt which the rats had made on it from eating
the good biscuit, and we drank water which was yellow and
stinking. We also ate the ox hides which were under the mainsail; they were very hard on account of the sun, rain and wind
and we left them four or five days in the sea, and then we put
them a little on the embers, and so ate them; also the sawdust
of wood, and rats which cost half a ducat apiece, moreover
enough of them were not to be caught." In consequence of
this diagonal north-westerly course their first landfall was the
group called by Magellan the Islands of Lateen Sails, later
known as the Ladrones or Isles of Thieves, and today as the
Marianas, from Maria Anna the queen of Philip IV. Les
Jardines, others called them, from the luxuriant vegetation of
Tinian and Guam. Thence Magellan continued west and somewhat south to Cebu in the central Philippines. At a neighbouring islet he was killed by savages whilst covering the retreat
of his men on September 27, 1521. His second in command,
Sebastian del Cano, took the little *Victoria* home to Seville the
next year with a cargo of 26 tons of cloves. The *Trinidad*, which
also crossed the Pacific, tried to regain America and disappeared.

The voyage was made and geographers like Ramusio extolled
the feat of men who excelled the Argonauts. But the aim of the
voyage—a shorter route to the Spice Islands—had been proved
illusory. Compared with the Portuguese route round Africa, it
was too long and too hard for ships sailing from European ports.
But that did not deter the Emperor Charles V from pressing his
claim to the Philippines and the Moluccas to the south of them.
The Portuguese denied that they fell within the Spanish sphere,
as had been delimited by the Treaty of Tordesillas. The question was argued in full debate between the learned cosmographers and experienced pilots of both nations. The Philippines
had not yet been so named, and nobody knew where either they
or the Moluccas lay, since nobody could calculate their longitude.
The argument was long and inconclusive; "after two months'

wrangling," remarks the eighteenth-century historian in hi
acid style, "the assembly broke up in a manner less ceremoniou
than that in which it had met; the Spaniards announcin,
judgement in favour of themselves, and the Portuguese threat
ening to put to death every Spaniard that should be found i1
the Moluccas" (a generic name for the Spice Islands). A fev
years later the Emperor relinquished his claim to the Molucca
for the payment of 350,000 ducats down; but he was no
prepared to surrender the Philippines.

In order to establish a footing there before his rivals coul
set up their ubiquitous trading stations, several expeditions wer
fitted out, one of them under Sebastian Cabot. But the onl
one which reached the islands was that under Loayasa, wit
whom sailed the now famous Del Cano. They were the secon
expedition to pass the Straits, this time in the extremity of th
Fuegian winter. When they reached the Philippines th
Portuguese attacked them as they had threatened, so Corte
was ordered to send out a rescue party from a Mexican por
under Alvaro de Saavedra. Contact was made with Loayasa'
men, but their leader had been killed and the prospect of
permanent settlement was futile unless reinforcements coul
be brought from America. Saavedra, therefore, tried to sai
east to recross the ocean. Being ignorant of the wind systen
prevailing in the north Pacific, he straightway encountered hea
winds in the shape of the North-East Trades. Driven back t
the islands, he tried again by a more southerly route whicl
brought him to the north coast of New Guinea, recently dis
covered by the Portuguese and so named from a fancied re
semblance to the coast of African Guinea. Again he was drive1
back, and he himself died at sea.

This continued lack of success gave the South Seas a ba
name among Spanish sailors. Even among the adventurou
spirits of the *conquistadores* none could be found who was anxiou
to relinquish the easy money of Peru to challenge the myster
of the Pacific again. Balboa, its discoverer, had been beheaded
Magellan killed by savages; Loayasa and Saavedra perished o1
the farther shore; one died raving, and another had turne

enegado and become a Mohammedan. Had a leader stepped
orward at this time he would never have manned a ship, for the
trength of ancient geographical superstitions was intensified by
uch facts.

So matters stood for nearly half a century. By now Pizarro
vas dead and there was chaos in Peru. The old Emperor was
lead too, disillusioned with the vanity of earthly things, and
 King Philip reigned in his stead. His Portuguese rival was far
oo content with the profits drawn from a royal monopoly in
pices in the Moluccas to venture farther east. Elsewhere in
Europe religious wars and the arguments of angry theologians
ttracted more attention than the possibilities of exploring un-
harted seas. After a half-hearted attempt to discover a northern
assage to Cathay in the reign of Henry VII, the English seemed
o have given up maritime enterprise in that direction, and their
ew queen was as yet too uncertain of her position to support
uch ventures. But the lust for gold remained a motive of
ndiminished strength; gold being, as Columbus said, "a most
xcellent thing, for by its possession men are enabled to have
ll that they would possess in this world and the means by which
hey may deliver souls from purgatory in the next." The mines
f Peru, indeed, provided enough silver for the most avaricious
aste, but gold in similar quantities was still lacking, and gold
vas said to be found in the Philippines; alternatively, it was
hought that the philosopher's stone might be discovered there.

One of the *hidalgos* who sailed to the Philippines with
Loayasa had been fortunate enough to return home in a Portu-
uese carrack. His name was Andres de Urdaneta. After a
istinguished career in New Spain as sailor, soldier, and cosmo-
rapher he joined the Augustinian Order. The friars exhibited
heir usual missionary zeal when, in 1565, forty years after
Loayasa's expedition, Philip suggested another attempt to
olonise the islands, this time under the command of Miguel
Lopez de Legaspe. Urdaneta was asked to accompany him as
dviser, since by reason of his vows he could not command a
hip. They were to sail from a Mexican port with a complement
f "holy guides to unfurl and wave the banners of Christ in the

remotest parts of these islands and drive the devil from the tyrannical possession which he had held so many ages, usurping to himself the adoration of those people." The sincere desire to propagate the truths of the Catholic faith was a motive almost as strong as the lust for gold in the great age of Spanish expansion. That is why friars sailed in every ship on a voyage of discovery, and that is why they often slaughtered the obstinate pagans with such insensate cruelty.

The ocean was crossed without incident owing to the North East Trades. Contrary to the advice of Urdaneta to turn aside to New Guinea or Guam, Legaspe held on for the Philippines to found settlements at Cebu and Manila. He remained in those parts for six years to establish a lasting colony under the slogan of *Predicar, Pacificar y Poblar*. The Spaniards prayed a great deal, but far from pacifying the islands they were soon in conflict with the natives, on whom they inflicted the same unholy cruelties as those their brethren used in the New World. Nor could they populate the settlement without the discovery of a safe and easy return route. Without access to America the pioneers remained cut off at the extremity of the known world, unable to fetch supplies, unable to introduce new blood, unable to export those products which alone gave value to the new colony.

The credit for the discovery of the route by which the Manila galleons were to sail to and fro between Mexico and the Philippines for the next three centuries has, until recently, been given to Urdaneta. The romantic reputation of the sailor-friar was successfully built up by monkish historians because his rival for the honour was a disreputable character, though of equally high birth. The latter's name was Arellano, and he too was one of Legaspe's comrades, but he sailed early without his commander's permission both on the voyage out and on the voyage home, probably in order to claim the reward of discovery. His log remains in a mutilated state and much of its contents is apparently sheer fiction; none the less it seems clear that he left the Philippines on the voyage home before Urdaneta did and reached Acapulco on the Mexican coast a month before him

The course followed was nearly the same in both cases. It was by now obvious that the prevalent wind in the latitude of the Philippines was easterly, but by sailing about midsummer the south-west monsoon could be utilised to carry ships to the Marianas. Thence they continued north to about latitude 40°, where, swept along by the Black Stream which runs up the coast of Japan, they entered the limits of the Westerlies. Shaping their course east across "a wide sea where ships can run free with any weather," they made a landfall somewhere in northern California, whence they ran down the coast to Acapulco. The voyage out only took eighty days, but the far more difficult return journey took anything up to six months. West with the North-East Trades, and east with the Westerlies, leaving New Spain early in the year and returning at the end of June when the monsoon sets in, such was the circular Manila route which Drake in the sixteenth and Anson in the eighteenth century tried to interrupt.

As far as spices and gold were concerned the Philippines were a disappointment to the colonists, for there was nothing but cinnamon and a few nuggets washed down by mountain streams. Contact with the Chinese proved more fruitful, so that by the time Drake was in those waters the trade was worth a million *pesos* a year. The cargo of the first two galleons in 1573 consisted of 3184 oz. of gold, 312 quintals (about a cwt.) of cinnamon, 712 pieces of silk, 32,300 pieces of gilt porcelain and a great deal of cotton thread. De Morga, the contemporary historian of the islands, adds a fine sounding list of luxury goods which includes velvets, embroidered brocades, ivory, jewels, dried fruits, "and even caged birds, some of which talk and sing, and they make them play a thousand tricks."

By that date the exploration of the northern Pacific was well advanced. Some of the scattered islets of the Marshall, Gilbert and Caroline groups, which lie to the south of the outward route of the galleons, were discovered one by one as ships were driven off their course. Over the discovery of the most important group—the Hawaiian Islands, lying inside the limits of the regular wind belts—there hangs an impenetrable mystery.

The natives have a legend that a Spanish ship was wrecked there in the sixteenth century; a map at Madrid has given rise to the suggestion that a certain Gaetano touched there about the middle of the century; but in the absence of further evidence conjecture is futile. To all intents and purposes they remained undiscovered until Cook found them and named them the Sandwich Isles.

On the other hand, only one island had been discovered in the southern part of the ocean, and that was Juan Fernandez, off the coast of Chile. Another mystery surrounds the identity of its discoverer, for our chief authority is a South American lawyer named Arias, who, about the year 1620, wrote a plea for the discovery of the "Austral land" before "the English and Dutch heretics, who are instigated by the Devil," got there first. According to him Fernandez, a soldier in Pizarro's army, attempted to find a quicker route from Callao to Valparaiso in 1563 by standing farther out into the ocean. By so doing he found the island which bears his name, together with Mas-a-fuera ("more without"). At a later date, according to Arias, he sailed due west along the fortieth parallel and after many days saw a coast "which, as far as they could judge, appeared to be *tierra firme*, the land fertile and pleasant, inhabited by white people, well made, of our own stature, dressed with good woven cloth, and peaceable and kind. . . . They were fully content with having discovered the coast of this great continent, so much desired." New Zealand is the only country which satisfies this description; even there early travellers found the Maoris far from peaceable. Like Gaetano's voyage, this second voyage by Fernandez must be dismissed as an invention. And unfortunately for Arias, the Dutch and English heretics succeeded in establishing "the poisonous venom of their apostasy" in the southern hemisphere because his advice was not taken.

Thus by the time the *Golden Hind* entered the Pacific the northern ocean had been crossed and recrossed a number of times, and Drake was able to use captured Spanish charts. What remained uncertain was its breadth. Accurate cartography being out of the question with the navigational instruments then in use, political prejudice made matters worse. The Spaniards tried to minimise the width of the ocean in order to bring the Philippines within their sphere of influence. The Portuguese exaggerated it with the same end in view, adding discouraging remarks about fogs and shoals and cannibals. In a Vespucci *mappemonde* made soon after the return of Magellan's expedition the Marianas are marked 110° from Panama instead of 155°, with the Philippines as two large islands a little farther west. In the standard maps of Ortelius and Mercator of half a century later the distance is reckoned at about 1500 leagues; Spanish pilots knew that it was more than 1750, and Portuguese politicians put it at 2000. Indeed the map from the first edition of Ortelius' famous atlas, reproduced as the frontispiece of this book, shows a fantastic under-estimation of the distance between North America and Japan. Furthermore, every nation had its own ideas as to what constituted a league, the Spanish reckoning it as three miles, the English as four and the French as two. An apparently academic question was a matter of life and death to seamen, since their food supply depended on the estimated duration of the voyage. Until accurate charts and maps were available, until the wind system was properly understood, the crossing of the northern sea remained dangerous, even though there was a known route. But in the southern part gigantic terrors loomed, because it was there that explorers and geographers, for two centuries to come, invented more than they discovered.

HOW THE SOLOMONS WERE FOUND AND LOST

THROUGHOUT the sixteenth, seventeenth and for most of the eighteenth century there persisted a belief that an undiscovered continent lay in the southernmost parts of the Pacific and Atlantic oceans. It is confidently marked in most of the *mappamundi* of the period stretching vaguely across the lower portions of the globe (see the Ortelius maps of 1570 and 1589, pp. 1, 26). Variously named *Terra Australis Incognita*, or *nondum cognita*, or *Terra Magellanica*, its northern coastline runs diagonally from somewhere in the latitude of Cape Horn to the coast of New Guinea, which was thought to be the northern part of what we call Australia. Bit by bit, successive explorers pare off pieces which were once shown as outlying parts of the mainland: the Falklands, Tierra del Fuego, Easter Island, New Guinea, New Zealand, Australia itself; but still it persists, a nebulous mass in an unknown sea, until finally Cook reduces *Terra Australis Incognita* to the confines of Antarctica. No geographical myth, not even the vain quest of the Northern Passages, has had such an attraction for the explorers of all nations.

The belief is of extreme antiquity. In one form or another it may be traced back to the writings of the Greek philosopher Theopompos, who flourished in the fourth century B.C. Nearly all later academic geographers sanctioned it because the idea is an eminently reasonable one. It was considered unlikely that so vast a stretch of water as the Pacific should exist without a land mass somewhere within its confines. Moreover, the symmetry of the globe demanded the existence of such a continent, for it was held that there must be an equivalent weight of land in the southern hemisphere to balance that known to exist in the northern, otherwise the globe itself would topple over to destruction amid the other stars. The curious thing about the

Plate I

THE WESTERN PACIFIC

Ortelius, *Theatrum Orbis Terrarum*, 1st ed. 1570

Plate II

MAG:

Miroir Oost et West Indical, 1621.

TS

is at the bottom of the chart

persistence of the belief is not its logic, but the fact that it was held far more strongly *after* men began to sail the Pacific than *before*. Behaim's globe of 1492 shows nothing to the south, since he prefers the alternative theory that the world is surrounded by water, *Fluvus Oceanus*. But the standard maps of the German school of Schöner and Sebastian Munster show signs of the continent, and the Flemish cartographers, Mercator and Ortelius, exaggerate it as *Terra Australis, Beach provincia aurifera*, extending it right across the southern parts of the globe and as far north as the Tropic of Capricorn. Ever since Marco Polo had written vaguely of Beach and Lochac (by which he presumably meant the Malay peninsula) the elusiveness of the continent, which borrowed these names for its western fringes, so preyed upon the minds of the successors of Magellan that they not merely assume its existence, but describe its shape, climate, vegetation and mineral wealth. Some go so far as to recommend it to their governments as a solution of the unemployment problem. If ever there was an example of wishful thinking, it was this.

At the time when the northern route to the Philippines was being worked out, one of the *conquistadores* of Peru, Don Pedro de Sarmiento de Gamboa, had no doubt about the existence of greater riches to the south. He based his belief on Inca tradition (on which subject he was the leading authority); the fact that his evidence was provided by slaves under pain of death, who would in such circumstances say anything to please their masters, did not diminish his confidence. He was by nature a bully, both cruel and credulous. His merciless, egotistic character does not endear him to us, but he was a skilful navigator and his ideas, had they been followed, might have changed the history of the Pacific.

A soldier who dabbled in Inca lore and the mysteries of cosmography obviously had the dangerous type of mind which it was the business of the Inquisition to safeguard. Early in his career in the New World he found himself the subject of the attention of the Holy Office about some matter of using magical ink and a ring with certain properties which women declared to be irresistible. He was sentenced to hear Mass in the cathedral stripped to his skin and to be banished from the Indies. On appeal to higher authority the latter part of the sentence was remitted, but it is likely that his eagerness to pursue the mirage in the west was partly due to anxiety to escape further questioning. According to his own brief account (or it may be an account written on his behalf) it was he who proposed an expedition "for the discovery of certain islands and a continent (*tierra firme*) lying to the west of Peru." He blames the other members of the expedition for not following his advice about the course to be followed, but their accounts never credit him with any such responsibility. To them he was no more than the captain of the smaller of the two ships which sailed from Callao on November 19, 1567.

At that date Sarmiento was a man of thirty-six. The command of the expedition was given to the Governor's nephew, Alvaro de Mendaña, a colourless young nobleman of only twenty-five. Evidently Sarmiento, who suggested it, hoped he could dominate Mendaña, but the latter preferred to trust Hernan Gallego, the chief pilot of the larger ship, or *Capitana* (more than twice the size of the *Victoria*), who had had some forty-five years' experience of the sea. Gallego was equally convinced that there were great discoveries to be made, but he did not intend that Sarmiento should show him how to make them. Everything must be done his own way, he argued, on the strength of the irrefutable argument that no one else knew anything about navigation. Two other important members of the crew were Gomez Catoira, the purser, who wrote the fullest account of the voyage, and Pedro de Ortega, Master of the Camp, a trustworthy soldier of a kindlier disposition than Sarmiento. Young Mendaña was in command of 150 men, of whom 70 were soldiers and the rest sailors or black slaves. There sailed with them four Franciscans "to convert all infidels" in the lands they proposed to discover and colonise.

On leaving Callao the course agreed on was west-south-west as far as latitude 23° S. But after three weeks without sight of land Gallego began to steer north-west till latitude 6° S. was reached. Sarmiento was furious. Already he had expostulated with the General for not stopping to investigate a cloudbank which he declared to be land. Now, in 15° S., Gallego was permitted to alter course on his own initiative. We may sympathise with Sarmiento, because had they continued on the agreed course they could not have failed to have discovered the Society Isles, where they would certainly have occupied Tahiti. As it was, they passed between the Low (or Tuamotu) and Marquesas groups and sighted nothing until, after many weeks, they fell in with one of the smallest of the Ellice group. Here, owing to Gallego's dilatoriness, they were caught in a current which prevented them from landing to refresh themselves. They continued west along parallel 6° S. until the current carried them south to nearly 8°. In this latitude, on their eightieth day at sea, Gallego saw something that looked like land. A sailor was ordered to the topmast and reported land fifteen leagues away. A flag was hoisted to notify the *Almiranta* astern of them, and everyone sang the *Te Deum*. The date was February 7, 1568.

As they approached, a wide bay with a dazzling sweep of sand and a fringe of palms opened before them. Mendaña named the land after their patroness, S. Ysabel, and the bay Bahia de la Estrella, for "just as we were entering the shallow water, we saw about the middle of the main-topsail a brilliant star, which we took to be a guide sent us by them (the three Magi, who had ever been our advocates) to show us the passage through the shallows." What they took to be main land was an island in the central Solomons.

Long before they dropped anchor powerful canoes with about thirty natives in each sped out to meet them. Mendaña threw red caps into the canoes by way of invitation to come on board, but the fuzzy-haired, blue-black savages dared not climb up the side until a sailor jumped overboard to guide them closer. Then a score swarmed up the side, ate the proffered meat and preserves, but spat out the wine with wry faces. Before long some were repeating the *Pater Noster* parrot fashion, to the delight of the friars, others were swarming up the rigging, or peering about for something to steal.

20291

As soon as the camp had been pitched under the palm trees the local chieftain appeared. According to native custom an introduction was effected by an exchange of names. "Bileban-Arra" said Mendaña. "Mendaña, Mendaña" repeated the savage for the rest of the afternoon, adding an assurance that food would be sent along the next day. But the appetites of a hundred and fifty voracious Spaniards soon taxed his generosity. Mendaña saw that the problem of food could only be solved by an expedition into the interior. While Gallego was set to build a five-ton brigantine for coastal exploration, Sarmiento was sent inland with sixteen soldiers. In the opinion of the General and his clerical advisers he would solve the problem uppermost in all their minds: was this land really a continent or merely an island?

Sarmiento did not penetrate far enough inland to find out anything beyond "indications of gold" and a surprising number of villages. So Ortega, the Master of the Camp, with thirty arquebusiers, fifteen soldiers and fifteen baggage boys, was instructed to climb the range they could discern in the distance. With native guides they set off through swamp and jungle to the stony path which climbed steeply up the foothills. At intervals groups of stalwart savages emerged from the undergrowth to persuade them to return, but they pressed on, sweating, swearing and stumbling, until they reached the top. By this time several hundred natives had come in from surrounding villages. With patient, friendly gestures Ortega asked for water, but none was brought. He began to threaten, and ordered four shots to be fired at a tree to impress the crowd. At this their guide tried to slip away, but Ortega caught him and held him squirming. Immediately the attitude of the natives became more threatening, several of the warriors, hideously streaked with white, brandishing their clubs and dancing about in warlike postures. Outfacing them stood the impassive square of Spaniards, their matches smouldering, their arquebuses loaded. As evening fell the crowd scattered and Ortega was able to question the guide more closely. He asked if there was any sea to the west; for answer the man drew a plan of an island in the dust and his information was confirmed next morning, though he himself had wriggled out of his bonds and disappeared. Ortega and his men were standing on the crest of the ridge which runs up the western side of the island. Far below, the white thread of surf breaking on the shore showed them that their continent was still to seek.

The return was more difficult. Without a guide they had to traverse thickly wooded and hostile country. Several times they were ambushed with sticks and arrows. Arquebuses were fired into the surrounding jungle, huts were burnt in revenge. But they returned without serious casualties, and it was not till the present century, when the Solomons came under British rule, that white men ever climbed those hills again.

Evidently the natives bore no malice for what had occurred, because a few days later they made a friendly if tactless gesture. A canoe came round the point and paddled close inshore opposite the camp. One of the crew stood up, holding in his hands what looked like a haunch of meat, shouting "Eat, eat!" A negro slave was sent to fetch the present. He returned with a human shoulder and arm. "It seemed to be a boy who had a small hand and a thin arm. We were all struck with great wonder and pity, to see so much cruelty and so strange a thing, such as we had never seen nor heard of; for though many had seen Indians eating human flesh, yet no one had ever heard of it being offered to anybody." The filthy object was immediately buried with gestures of extreme disapproval, indeed Mendaña found it difficult to restrain his men from firing on the canoe. Hurt and surprised, the natives paddled off to join the cannibal feast which had already begun, to judge from the smoke which could be seen rising from behind the trees. In spite of the pacific policy urged by Mendaña and the friars, who seem to have been more humane than most of their compatriots, the minds of the soldiers hardened after this incident, and they gladly obeyed Sarmiento's orders to treat the savages as they treated the Incas at home, to burn and massacre on the slightest provocation.

Now that S. Ysabel had been found to be an island the

brigantine was sent on the first of her exploratory cruises. In
the course of three such expeditions Ortega and Gallego visited
most of the southern Solomons—Guadalcanal (which Ortega
named after the place of his birth and spelt thus), San Cristoval
Malaita (literally "There is Mala"). Of the northern island
they only sighted Choiseul in the course of a circumnavigation
of S. Ysabel, and left it without a name.

In consequence of renewed quarrels with the natives
Mendaña found food again running short, so he decided to
move camp south to the island of Guadalcanal. Here the same
story was repeated: the Spaniards were welcomed; they
demanded food and water; when these were not forthcoming
in sufficient quantity kidnapping and shooting began, watering
parties were attacked in revenge, shore parties ambushed,
Sarmiento burnt a few villages, and it was decided to move
camp once more—this time to San Cristoval.

Here, on August 7, Mendaña called a meeting to decide
what to do next. Should they remain where they were and
establish a colony? Return home? Seek for further signs of
the continent? Young and inexperienced, and of a far from
autocratic temperament, Mendaña willingly followed his instructions to call a general council whenever future policy had
to be decided on. Fifty-eight Spaniards attended. As befitted
his position, Mendaña opened the debate by pointing out that
the brigantine had found no signs of land to the southward, but
that as they still had enough provisions for five months at sea
they should steer north "to go and discover more lands."
Gallego spoke next. He said that he would leave the question
of settlement to the soldiers, but speaking as Chief Pilot he must
point out that the ships were not in a fit condition for further
voyages of discovery. Sarmiento followed with emphatic advice
to settle. Many soldiers agreed with him, but Ortega and the
friars were for returning, because they felt the King never
intended them to settle at an island so much farther west than
had originally been anticipated. In spite of what Sarmiento
says, this seems to have been the opinion of the majority, and
Mendaña accepted the verdict. He therefore ordered the brig-

antine to be burnt and both ships to set sail east, a course which he thought would bring them back to Peru in a shorter time. The pilots protested vehemently. Experience had shown that the prevailing winds in those latitudes were easterly, and it was madness to try a dead beat right across the Pacific. But Mendaña insisted and for five days they tried in vain to beat to windward; then the wind shifted a little and they lost sight of San Cristoval. From that day the Solomons were lost once more, until Carteret discovered them accidentally almost exactly two hundred years later. In most of the maps issued during the latter part of the sixteenth century they are correctly placed, but then they begin to wander anywhere between two and eight thousand miles west of Peru. On a number of later maps they have disappeared altogether (see below, p. 162). Head winds continued to prevail. Sarmiento grumbled because, once again, he had been over-ruled. If they had to leave the islands they should, in his view, have sailed south-west "in search of the other lands he wished to discover at the beginning." Had this course been adopted they would have discovered the Queensland coast, and no one can say how history might have been altered.

Gallego was equally obstinate in his opposition to the easterly course. Mendaña endeavoured to pacify him with the assurance that the wind would change with the moon, but he would not believe it. He continued his grumbling in the forecastle with the unanswerable argument: "the landsman reasons but the seaman navigates." Many soldiers agreed with him, and since "they did not understand the matter" they urged him to try once more to persuade Mendaña. Catching the general disaffection, the sailors refused to set the sails properly, and when they were scolded muttered something about not having enough to eat. Mendaña remained obdurate and told the pilots "they must not cross the Line on any account."

In despair Gallego rowed over to the *Almiranta* to enlist further support. A general petition was drafted, signed by Ortega, Sarmiento, Catoira and all the pilots. This was attached to a line and thrown on board the quarter-deck of the *Capitana*.

Fearing a mutiny, the General at length agreed, though he insisted on a typically weak compromise: the ships were to steer north, but course must be altered to south-east whenever the wind served. After a few days of this Gallego had to protest again, since tacking to and fro in this manner merely exhausted their provisions. Fortunately for their lives, Mendaña in the end gave in. They would certainly never have seen home again if he had been allowed to have his way.

Skirting the outlying atolls of the Marshall and Gilbert groups north of the line, they continued on their northerly course until, on October 1, 1568, they sighted Wake, the loneliest of all Pacific islands—a small bare atoll only a few feet above the surface of the ocean which surrounds it for thousands of miles on every side. San Francisco, as they called it, was not seen again until the *Prince William Henry* rediscovered it in 1796. Even then few had ever heard of it before the Japanese attack in 1941.

A fortnight later they began to turn east in latitude 32° N within the limit of the Westerlies. The latent hostility between Mendaña and Sarmiento now took a more dramatic turn. The latter's motives are not clear: all we know is that for some days his ship began to develop a suspicious tendency to part company with the *Capitana* by drifting to leeward. Several times Mendaña hailed her and ordered her to bear up; "they always said that they were doing their best and could do no more." On the night of October 17 she was out of sight. All next day the *Capitana* lay to, wasting the fine weather, until just before nightfall they caught a glimpse of her hull down on the horizon. By next morning she had disappeared once more. Of course Sarmiento claims that he was deserted, and says that if it had not been for his own efforts the ship would have been cast away in mid-ocean.

Mendaña's crew had cause for more serious anxiety a few hours later. The wind suddenly freshened so that they had to furl the mainsail and lie to with only the stern sail set. Then, without warning, they were caught by a sudden gust of hurricane force. In a moment the decks were awash and the ship

eeled over to port on her beam ends. Mendaña ran on deck
o order the ship's boat to be cut away, leaving the friars to chant
he Creed to the panic-stricken mob below. But cutting the
oat loose did not right the ship. He then gave an order to cut
own the mainmast. The pilots objected that if that was done
hey could never make port. For once Mendaña was adamant.
He told a sailor standing by with an axe in his hand to cut down
he mast, whatever the pilots said. "When he had struck the
mast twice it went overboard with all the rigging, maintop,
ards and sails." At this the ship righted a little and they tried
o set a foresail, but it was blown out in a moment. Catoira
was sent forward "to see if it was possible to make a little sail
with a blanket. . . . When I reached the prow I found three
or four negroes and several sailors half dead: by sheer cudgelling
made them hold the blanket each on his side, and as they did
o the ship gradually righted, and rising from a trough of the
ea, fell slowly to leeward notwithstanding that the storm was
till severe."

For three days it blew. In all Gallego's years at sea he had
never seen the like of it. After it died down recriminations
began. Mendaña was blamed for wasting the fine weather
waiting for the *Almiranta*. There was still no sign of land, all
he biscuit was eaten and the water was putrid with cockroaches.
Men died daily of scurvy, their gums swelling over their teeth,
heir bones brittle with disease; others, gambling away their
water rations, went mad or blind. The soldiers demanded an
immediate return to the Philippines. That was madness, said
Mendaña, in view of their shortage of provisions. They told
him to consult the pilots. He answered that it was because he
had listened to them in the first place that they were now in
his condition. He assured them that land could not be far off.
"They replied that they had no longer any faith in charts and
papers." Mutiny looked like breaking out at any moment, for
"they gathered in knots and circles discussing how I could not
only be prevailed upon to put back, but forced to do so."

What happened next was so opportune that one is not surprised Mendaña calls it a miracle. "I saw floating upon the

water towards the ship a large piece of timber, very clean an
without bark; and pointing it out to the men, I said 'See wha
you would have done; we have reached land!'" And the nex
day a fair wind sprang up and there came a shower of rain
which they soaked up with sheets and drank greedily.

On December 15, after being continuously at sea for fou
months, Gallego called his "best friends," Mendaña and Catoira
to the poop. He pointed out something on the horizon whicl
might be land, or it might be another bank of cloud. The
dared not tell the rest until, next morning, there was no doub
about it. Gallego told Catoira he could claim the reward fo
announcing the good news, and "I began to shout 'Land
Land!' Then all rushed up from below and began to embrac
me and each other, weeping for joy, and all rendering thank
unto Our Lord."

Their landfall was somewhere on the coast of Lower Cali
fornia. Running south they opened the bay of Colima, wher
they anchored. The very next day a derelict ship loomed u
from the west; as she came closer they identified her to thei
joy as the *Almiranta*, dismasted like themselves by the hurri
cane, and with not a drop of water on board. It was forty day
before they could continue south to the Mexican ports, wher
they were at first refused entry because they were mistaken fo
"Lutherans" and "strange Scottish people," such was the fea
the English and French privateers under Hawkins had awakene
in the breasts of even these western colonists.

Ever since the *Almiranta* had rejoined there was open hos
tility between Mendaña and Sarmiento. To judge from th
dark hints dropped in various narratives, Sarmiento was tryin
to get a warrant against Ortega for depriving him of the com
mand of the ship. When the *Almiranta* began to forge ahea
again Mendaña was convinced she was trying to desert a secon
time. At the next port of call Sarmiento was put ashore unde
arrest, and the others sailed for Peru without him. He mus
have been aware of his danger if Mendaña succeeded in bringin
a charge against him in Peru, so he managed to escape with
slave. Fortunately for him a new Governor took office tw

months after Mendaña's return, with the result that the fugitive was reinstated and Mendaña went unheard and unrewarded.

But Sarmiento's later career was so uniformly unfortunate that many said he suffered from the curse of the Incas, the last of whom he personally hunted down and brought to execution. When Drake appeared in the Pacific he was sent in chase. Returning without success, he was sent to fortify the Straits of Magellan to block the raider's possible return by that route. His attempt to establish a settlement in that inhospitable land was a tragic fiasco. Cavendish at length took off the miserable remnant from what he called Port Famine, "where they died like so many dogs, in their houses, in great numbers, and the stench of the putrefying carcasses infecting those that survived, they were forced to quit the town with one consent, and go rambling upon the sea coasts living upon leaves and roots and sea herbs, or what animals they at any time happily caught." Long before that Sarmiento had been captured at sea, first by the English and then, after paying a heavy ransom, by the French. At least he was the first to attempt to chart the Straits, and his name remains to this day as that of the highest peak in Tierra del Fuego, as does the name Cavendish gave to his ill-fated settlement.

Mendaña met with no better success, now that his uncle was out of office. Official opinion was not impressed by his discoveries. "On the 8th of February," wrote the provincial Licentiate to the King, "there put into the port of Santiago near Colima, two battered ships without masts or victuals, which had set out from the port of Lima in Peru, in quest of the Western Islands, the Solomon Islands, and New Guinea. . . . In my opinion they (the islands discovered) were of little importance, although they say they heard of better lands; for in the course of these discoveries they found no specimens of spices, nor of gold and silver, nor of merchandise, nor of any other source of profit, and all the people were naked savages."

The interesting thing about the letter is that this is the first time the name "Solomon Islands" is used to describe what had been discovered. How did the name originate? None of the narratives of the expedition refers to them in these terms though Mendaña and his men named particular islands such a Ysabel, Guadalcanal, San Cristoval. It has been suggested that popular opinion on the Pacific water-fronts was excited by the highly coloured stories of the survivors, so that these western islands came to be identified in popular imagination with Solomon's fabled Ophir, whence he drew inexhaustible store of gold. But the date of the letter is March 20, 1569, and Mendaña only arrived at the beginning of February, too short an interval for a popular nickname to become current in official circles. Possibly the islands were already known by that name by the members of the crew. Anyhow, like King Solomon's Mines, the Solomon Islands came to represent gold and frankincense and myrrh, and so they remained for centuries, a golden promise of that far wider and insubstantial vision—*Terra Australis Incognita*.

III

THE TRAGEDY OF THE ISLANDS WHERE
SOLOMON WAS WANTING

SINCE the value of his discoveries was not appreciated by the
officials of New Spain, Mendaña returned home with his uncle
to enlist the interest of the Court. After some delay he obtained,
in 1574, permission to fit out another expedition, but before he
could embark he was imprisoned on a minor charge.

In the tale of his misfortunes there was none so serious as
this, for that was the date when the English first began to take
an interest in the Pacific. For some time past the possibility of
exploration in that direction had intrigued propagandists of
maritime enterprise. Here might be a shorter route to the
Spice Islands, either by the Straits of Anian (the North-West
Passage), or by the Straits of Magellan. To Spanish claims of
monopoly the English replied with the doctrine of the Freedom
of the Seas in its original form: "the maine Ocean by right is
the Lord's alone," wrote Drake's nephew, "and by nature left
free for all men to deale withall, as very sufficient for all men's
use, and large enough for all men's industry." Robert Thorne
in the reign of Henry VIII had provided a proud motto for the
Elizabethans: "There is no land unhabitable, nor sea un-
navigable." Now news of Mendaña's discoveries, with an assurance of the existence of a North-West Passage, was brought
home by Henry Hawks, a trader in New Mexico before his im-
prisonment at the hands of the Inquisition. Acting on his
information, a group of Devon gentlemen, of whom Sir Richard
Grenville was the most noteworthy, formed a project for the
exploration of the southern route and the annexation of *Terra
Australis*, in opposition to the attempts about to be made by
Frobisher and his supporters to explore the northern route.

But Grenville chose the wrong time to petition the Queen
for her permission. At the moment she wanted peace with

Spain. Three years later she changed her mind and accepted
Drake's revival of the project. There were so many discussions
and so many schemes afoot to satisfy this or that interest that
only Drake and his royal mistress knew exactly what was to be
done when he sailed in 1577. The proliferations of the original
plan included the colonisation of *Terra Australis*, the opening
up of a route to the Moluccas, the search for a western exit of
the North-West Passage (said to exist about the latitude of
California, and usually called the Strait of Anian), and the
possibility of establishing a base there. Mendaña had proved
the potentialities of the Pacific: it remained for the English to
get there first.

Probably with the Queen's connivance, Drake threw all these
schemes overboard, preferring to take advantage of the easy
money offered along the undefended coast of South America.
There is no need to add to the descriptions of that wonderful
voyage: we may be sure that until the end of time popular
novelists will continue to try their hand at it. Geographically
speaking, the results were disappointing. Drake may or may
not have searched for the western exit of the Strait of Anian,
in any case the search was vain. What is more important is to
determine exactly what he discovered earlier, in consequence of
being driven off his course by the tremendous gales encountered
when he emerged from the Straits of Magellan. According to
different accounts he was driven south to 55°, 56° or 57°.
Precisely where did that curious scene take place when he lay
on his face and stretched his hands over a cliff, claiming that no
man had ever been so far south as he? The old view that the
so-called Elizabeth Island was Cape Horn or thereabouts has been
effectively exploded by recent writers. One of them identifies
the spot with the now submerged reef called Burnham Bank.
Another with Henderson Island, at the southern end of the
channel dividing Tierra del Fuego. According to the Portuguese pilot's log, which has survived whereas Drake's has disappeared, he was never driven far enough east to discover Cape
Horn. But from what he appears to have told Richard Hawkins
it is clear that he guessed Tierra del Fuego was an island and

not part of a southern continent, as had been supposed hitherto: "The uttermost cape or headland of all these islands, stands near in the 56th degree; without which there is no main nor island to be seen to the Southward but the Atlantic Ocean and the South Sea meet in a large and free scope. It hath been a dream through many ages that these islands have been a main, and that it hath been *terra incognita*, for howsoever the maps and general descriptions of cosmographers, either upon the desirable reports of other men, or the deceitful imaginations of themselves (supposing never herein to be corrected), have set it down, yet it is true that before this time, it was never discovered, or certainly known by any traveller that we have heard of."

Plain enough; but unfortunately that was written twelve years after the true discovery of the Horn by Schouten and Le Maire in 1616 in a book openly propagandist in intention. All we can say is that Drake guessed, and guessed rightly, at the possibility of such a route, thereby cutting the first slice off the unknown continent. Perhaps he kept silence because the new route was regarded as a state secret; perhaps because he was not certain of its existence. Some maps published after his voyage omit *Terra Australis*, others do not; the majority, even while they accept the fact that Tierra del Fuego is an island, refuse to banish the possibility of such a continent farther west, where Drake had not sailed.

With the incursion of Drake into the Pacific all thoughts of following up Mendaña's discovery had to be postponed. Of the many other Elizabethans who tried to repeat the success of a voyage which became the talk of Europe because it heralded the appearance of a new maritime power, only Cavendish succeeded, and even he failed to penetrate the Straits on his second voyage. In 1593 Sir Richard Hawkins tried again, but was captured off Callao, the port of Lima. From that date for close on a hundred years no English ship sailed into those waters.

With the last English intruder in prison the people of New Spain breathed freely again, and Mendaña found the atmosphere more propitious for a renewed undertaking to settle the

Solomons. Fortunately for him, he sailed a few months before
Drake's last raid on the Indies in 1595.

Mendaña had discovered the Solomons at the age of twenty-
six. He was now a man of fifty-three, dignified with the title of
Adelantado, encumbered with an unpleasant wife and three
brothers-in-law, all of whom insisted on sailing with him. One
of them, Don Lorenzo, was appointed Admiral, and no doubt
looked forward to making a family fortune. Why Dona Isabel
de Barreto (the "Governess") sailed one cannot imagine, unless
it was to take her place at her husband's side when he became
Governor of the Solomon Islands. A worse type of pioneer it is
impossible to imagine. Indeed, the combination of avarice,
vanity and stupidity in her person nearly ruined the whole
expedition.

Just as he had placed implicit trust in Gallego on his first
expedition, so in 1595 Mendaña left all navigational problems to
his new pilot, Pedro Fernandez de Quiros—a loyal, intelligent
young Portuguese of the utmost importance in the history of the
exploration of the Pacific. A man of obscure origins and little
education, born in the slums of Lisbon, and only thirty years old,
circumstances presented him with responsibilities far graver
than his position or experience had prepared him for. He was
imaginative, talkative, devout and unswerving in loyalty to his
superiors, but he suffered from the most serious fault an explorer
can have—he was no leader of men. However much he talked,
no one listened to him.

Of the 378 persons Mendaña commanded in his four ships—
two large ones, a galeot and a "frigate"—a great number were
of a thoroughly undesirable type for a project of this scope. The
prospect of colonising islands, whose attractions had been grossly
exaggerated by popular report, attracted many soldiers of fortune
who had so far failed to make their fortunes, together with a
number of women, mostly of ill fame. Some of the worst of
both classes were put ashore before they finally sailed; among
the remainder there were fifteen marriages before they had
been at sea a month. As on the previous expedition, the soldiers,
drawn from a higher caste than the sailors, caused the trouble

The Master of the Camp was their ringleader. Don Pedro Merino Manrique typified Spanish soldiery at its worst: brutal, domineering, quarrelsome and impetuous, in spite of his sixty years and white hair. As soon as he came on board trouble began. He immediately found fault with the boatswain, though it was none of his business.

"The Master of the Camp is severe," agreed Dona Isabel when the Pilot complained of his interference. "If that is the way in which he asserts his position, he may have a prosperous end, though I am far from thinking so."

"Oh look! What have we here?" Manrique replied impudently when she reprimanded him. "Know me!" he shouted to Quiros who was standing by. "Understand that I am the Master of the Camp, and if we sail together on one ship, and I ordered the ship to be run on some rocks, what would you do?"

"When that time comes I shall do what seems to me to be best," answered Quiros quietly; "and in this fleet I do not recognise any other head but the Adelantado, who has delivered the charge of this ship to me, whose Captain I am."

Disorder broke out at every port at which they touched to make up their complement. Manrique's voice was always to be heard, hectoring the sailors, introducing friends and followers to whom he sold official positions, quarrelling with the Franciscan Vicar himself. Naturally the disorderly element on board followed his example. Voices were raised in anger, hands laid on sword hilts, gimlet holes bored in the ship's bottom, till even the loyal Quiros begged to be put on shore rather than cross the South Sea in such company. Mendaña threw his arms around his neck and begged him to remain: their goal was clearly marked in Gallego's chart at only 1450 leagues away; everything would be all right if he omitted to mark any land on his chart between 7° and 12° S., "lest some ship should steer to or desert to it." So much for the lesson that Sarmiento had taught him.

The metal of which his soldiery was made became evident at their first discovery, the lovely Marquesas Islands, named by Mendaña after his friend the Viceroy, Las Marquesas de

Mendoza. He mistook them at first for the Solomons, though they are only a thousand leagues from Peru. The inhabitants proved friendly, though, as always, inclined to pilfer. An arquebus was fired to frighten them away from the ship, and when one of them refused to let go the tow rope a soldier chopped his hand off. Later another soldier, losing his nerve when surrounded with canoes, fired and killed. Quiros told him it was a pity he had not fired into the sea. "On the contrary," replied the soldier, "I acted as I did lest I should lose my reputation as a good marksman"; besides, wounds "so fierce and ugly" as those made by bullets would prove a powerful deterrent. A few days later Quiros managed to snatch the arquebus out of the hands of a soldier who was about to fire simply because, as he admitted, "he liked to kill." "It is not right that you should show such readiness to cause the death of men," Quiros expostulated. "What harm have the natives done to you that you should treat them with such cruelty? It is not valorous to show yourself a lion amongst lambs, nor to kill whom it takes your fancy." Clearly, the Pilot cannot have lived long in Peru. Having tried in vain to persuade some of the men to settle there, Mendaña sailed on west, leaving a few corpses dangling from the trees to commemorate the new discovery.

As they continued along parallel 10° S. day after day without sighting anything but uninhabited atolls, the temper of the undisciplined soldiery grew worse and the class distinction between soldiers and sailors, which did so much to impair Spanish efficiency at sea, became sharper. The Chief Pilot was accused of having lost his way; it was said that the Adelantado had merely brought them there to drown them; some feared they would run on the coast of Grand Tartary if they continued much farther in that direction; everyone agreed that "this business is very different from what it was supposed to be. Here there is neither honour nor life. . . ."

On September 7, 1595, they ran into a thick mist, in which the *Almiranta* disappeared, never to be seen again. But an hour before nightfall the fog lifted and there, right ahead of the

Capitana, less than a league away, was the smoking volcano of Tinakula. Once again Mendaña mistook it for the Solomons; later he named the group the Islands of Santa Cruz.

He quickly made friends with the handsome savages, each with a red hibiscus flower in his hair, and made the usual exchange of names with Malope, their chief. Mirrors, beads, scissors were distributed and the natives taught without delay to make the sign of the Cross. Such simple civilities did not please the soldiers. Within a few days trouble began on shore, where the Master of the Camp was installed, Mendaña and his relations remaining on the ship. The Adelantado must have remembered with foreboding the trouble he had had thirty years ago in the Solomons. In an effort to prevent the inevitable predatory expedition he persuaded the shore party to set about clearing the jungle to lay the foundations of a permanent settlement. A few responded with enthusiasm, but the memory of Peruvian delights was not so easily exorcised. Before long the sort of petition Mendaña knew so well was produced, begging him to leave the place for "the islands he had talked about." A native or two was deliberately murdered to stir up trouble, and one scoundrel announced his pleasure at the approaching crisis in the words: "The Camp Master is my cock; all are afraid of him. Now things are ripening. Before long we shall see something, and before long we shall have liberty!"

Mendaña lay in his cabin sick with worry and malaria. He realised his authority was waning. Quiros begged him to take sterner measures before it was too late—this was after an attempt had been made on the Pilot's life, the culprit declaring that he was shooting at a bird. But Mendaña was never the man for that. So Quiros took it upon himself to visit the camp. An angry hum of questions greeted him. "Where have you brought us to? What place is this whence no man goes, and to which no man will return? Embark us and take us to seek those other islands, or take us to Peru, or some part where there are Christians!" Quiros' long and sarcastic reply was totally unsuited to the occasion. He pointed out that the greatest places must have their beginnings; did they expect cities, vineyards,

gardens ready made? All in vain. It was his first attempt to
impose his will on others, and, as he candidly admits, it was a
complete failure. "They went back to their old song—'Manila!
Manila! That is a land for Christians!'" "Come let us kill
him, for he is the cause of our being in this land," urged one
fellow, adding, with an oath, that he looked forward to drinking
out of his skull.

Back on board he found Dona Isabel thoroughly frightened.
She was trying to persuade her husband to kill the Master of the
Camp. If he didn't do it, she would do it herself. That night
the sick man called Quiros to his bedside and told him his plan.

Next morning there were shouts from the shore demanding
a boat. "Alas! Alas!" cried Dona Isabel, "they ask for a boat
to come and kill us!" The boat put off, but in it were the
Adelantado, shaking with fever, Quiros, the royal standard
bearer, and the captain of the galeot with a hatchet in his hand.
The brothers-in-law welcomed Mendaña as he stepped ashore,
and the party walked over to the Camp Master's tent, where
Manrique was having breakfast. He came out to meet them
without hat or coat. As soon as he saw his visitors he realised
his danger and called for a sword or dagger.

"Those who had to do the deed were arriving," writes
Quiros sombrely. "The Adelantado raised his eyes to heaven,
and giving a sigh, put his hand to his sword, saying: 'Long
live the King! Death to traitors!' Upon this one Juan Antonio
de la Roca took the Camp Master by the collar, and gave him
two stabs, one in the mouth and the other on the breast. Then
a sergeant, with a Bohemian knife, gave him another on the
side. The Camp Master cried 'Oh, gentlemen!' He turned
to get his sword, but the captain (of the galeot) with his wood-
knife, nearly cut off his right arm. He fell, saying 'Oh, leave
me time to confess!' One answered that 'there was no time.
You can well feel contrition.' The wretched man was palpi-
tating, stretched on the ground, and crying 'Jesu Maria!' A
good woman came up, and helped him to die in peace. One
with a kind heart did no more than draw out the sword,
and the woman gave it up. So the body was left and the

Adelantado approved the slaughter. . . . The Camp Master having expired, the drummer, coveting his clothes, left him naked."

It was the signal for a general massacre. One of Mendaña's relations seized a soldier, with whom he had been talking amicably a moment before, and stabbed him with his dagger. "For me? For me?" cried the wounded man, "What have I done?" Brushing Quiros aside as he attempted to intervene, Don Louis ran the man through with his sword. "Death to traitors!" he cried as he rushed into the next tent. "Kill them! Kill them! They deserve it more than the others!" Women came running out as the men rushed about like lunatics, shouting, swearing, killing.

Another boat was seen approaching from the ship. In it stood the Vicar, a lance in his hand, and the crew shouting "Death to traitors!" Then Dona Isabel and her sisters appeared, having heard the news from the captain of the galeot who, flourishing the blood-stained hatchet with which he had just chopped off a couple of heads, added, "Now you are mistress and marchioness and I am Captain!"

We know with what horror Quiros witnessed this "tragedy of the islands where Solomon was wanting." Mendaña was no Solomon, and that sigh of his as he gave the order to kill reveals his attitude clearly enough. At least the royal standard gave him the form of legality, and the Church was on his side too. The slaughter over, everyone was ordered to hear Mass, after which the Vicar told them "not to be scandalised at the deaths, for it was ordained." But the Adelantado returned to the ship sick in body and soul. The outrage he had countenanced, obviously at the instigation of his relatives, solved no problems. Indeed before it began a predatory expedition had started on its way to kill Malope. The friendly chief was shot in cold blood and his skull split with a hatchet. "He is well dead," announced the murderer on his return. "Is there anyone who wants to see my death?" Evidently he did not realise how the balance of power had shifted during the few hours he had been away. He was quickly disarmed and brought before the Adelantado in

chains.   Meanwhile Don Lorenzo had summoned the chaplain
from the hostile camp.

"Sir Captain," the priest protested, "what is it that you
want with me? Remember that I am a priest. Oh, for the
sake of the one God, do not kill me!"

"Come with me—just for a little," urged Don Lorenzo.

"Here! Here! I cannot go any farther," cried the un
happy man.

They had great difficulty in explaining to him that he wa
merely asked to confess Malope's murderer. "Let it be then a
God wills!" cried the victim. While he was on his knees before
his confessor a black slave cut off his head with one blow.

Mendaña himself was by now a dying man. Realising tha
his end was near he nominated Don Lorenzo as Captain
General and Dona Isabel as Governess. On October 18 he died
He was not a man of the heroic proportions of others who saile
beyond the sunset, but he showed a persistence in his searcl
after the islands that do not even bear his name which contrast
oddly with his diffident character. He seems out of place as th
leader of gold-lusting adventurers and tough *conquistadores*
Quiros' ambiguously worded obituary adds little to our insigh
into his shadowy personality: "He was a person zealous for th
honour of God and the service of the King, to whom all thing
ill done did not appear good, nor did those well done appear evil
He was very plain spoken, not diffuse in giving his reasons, an
he himself said he did not want arguments but deeds." Un
fortunately, most of his career was taken up by argument; a
Quiros adds, "it seemed to me that he might say with reason
that he knew more than he performed, yet he saw nothing
that passed by stealth."

They buried him with the honour befitting his rank, no
was his grave left for savages to rifle. When they departed the
took the coffin with them to Manila.

The epidemic from which their leader died swept through th
ship and the camp. Within a few weeks Don Lorenzo and th
Vicar were dead, and so many of the rank and file that a handfu
of natives could have overrun the settlement. It was obviou

nat the remnant must leave this "corner of Hell" or perish. o, leaving Santa Cruz "in the claws of the Devil," they set uil west-north-west in the direction of the Philippines. By ow Quiros was convinced that his predecessor had under-stimated the distance between Peru and the Solomons. He .ad, but not seriously so, and if Quiros had continued a hundred niles west he would have reached San Cristoval, which is in the ame latitude as Santa Cruz. Indeed he seems to have sighted he most easterly of the Solomons which he mistook for the coast f New Guinea. In what he calls latitude 11° S. he says he haped his course "to avoid New Guinea, which was very near, nd not to get among the islands." Again in 5° S., "we under-tood that New Guinea was close on board"—probably what he neant was Bougainville Island.

Continuing north-west in a heavy sea which buffeted the otten timbers of his ship, he crossed the line on what must be ccounted one of the most heroic of Pacific voyages. Without chart and without the authority of supreme command, he had o sail a crazy ship full of sick and discontented men across housands of miles of unknown sea, and this at the age of thirty. The mainmast of the *Capitana* was sprung, the timbers of the wo smaller ships were so rotten that he despaired of them daily, heir tackle rotten with rain and damp—some of the ropes had jeen spliced thirty-three times—their yards warped and their ails patched and torn. Worst of all, the Governess had to be onsulted at every turn, and on every point she showed herself a criminally stupid woman. The crew were still dying at the ate of two or three a day; there were not enough able men to noist the mainsail, which lay flapping in the waist while fever-tricken wretches crawled about the decks. "One of them said o the Chief Pilot, he was tired of being always tired and he vould rather die once than many times: they might as well hut their eyes and let the ship go to the bottom." The obvious :hing to do was to sink the two smaller ships and combine the :rews; but the Governess would not hear of it. She argued that as the Pilot had not paid for the ships he could have no say in what should be done with them, with the result that the

D

frigate was later found stranded with her sails set and all he
people dead, and the galeot made her way independently to th
Philippines. She remained in her cabin playing with the key
of the store-room, washing her clothes in drinking wate
"Cannot I do what I please with my own property?" she aske
petulantly, when Quiros begged her for the hundredth time fo
some relief for the famished men on deck. "It belongs to al
and it will go to all," he warned her; "it is your duty to curta
your allowance that the soldiers may not say that you wash you
clothes in their life blood." With sarcasm unusual in so loyal
man, he pointed out that at her age and in her situation sh
could not behave like Dido or Semiramis. No wonder he sus
pected her of planning his death afterwards.

At last they reached Guam in the Marianas, but it proved
disappointment because their tackle was so rotten they could nc
even hoist the boat away. After taking in what provisions h
could he set a course for Cap Espiritu Santo in the Philippine
across waters which, had he but known it, are the deepest in th
world. His navigation was so accurate that they soon sighte
the cape. "Soon we shall hear Mass and seek God," cried th
men, "there is no longer danger of death without confession
for that is a land where Christians dwell."

But the Pilot knew better. The coast was armoured with
reefs, he had no chart and no tackle for boat or anchor. Th
desperate men were on the verge of mutiny when he insiste
on skirting the coast. When he tried to force them to work the
"turned their backs without answering and made use of ba
language." As for the Governess, she washed her hands of al
responsibility: "in her retreat she appeared to be making
arrangements with death, a book of devotions in her hands, he
eyes turned to heaven, making ejaculations and as afflicted an
tearful as the rest."

Two miracles saved him. A breeze sprang up to carry then
down into an open bay, and a canoe put out in which there wa
a native pilot who had served Cavendish ten years previously
Provisions were collected and Quiros hoped that there would be
time to refit the ship, but now the Governess was all for reaching

Manila without delay. He was in despair. As he told the soldiers, "I know not what steps to take in order to bring this lady to reason." She knew that she had the whip hand, for her pilot could not disobey without risking trial on their return, and so they put to sea once more.

The next canoes they met with sheered off, because they had been warned not to approach strange ships, lest they should prove to be English. Again provisions ran short and again Quiros petitioned in vain for part at least of the twenty jars of water, the two sacks of flour, the calf, or the two pigs which remained on board. "Sir Captain, have you spent 40,000 dollars as I have on this expedition, or have these people undertaken it at their own charge?"

"My Lady, I spent my property, and each one spent what they had; many gave up their lives, and all expended all they knew. . . . That which belonged to the Adelantado, and that which belongs to your Ladyship, must be used for the necessities of the voyage." Driven to the limit of his loyalty, he threatened that the men would take the stores by force. At this she relented to the extent of giving up the calf, but she would not part with her pigs.

However, the end of that dreadful voyage was approaching, thanks to Quiros' skill as a navigator. A few miles out of Manila a boat met them with four Spaniards in it: they looked, he says cheerily, like 40,000 angels. When they came up the side they were horrified at the skeleton crew, their tattered clothes and famished eyes, their rotten sails and mouldy gear, the corpses lying in the scuppers because no one had the strength to throw them overboard.

"What do you bring us to eat? Oh, give us food, for we are mad with hunger and thirst!"

Catching sight of the two pigs, the newcomers asked, "Why do they not kill those pigs?"

"They belong to the Governess."

"What the Devil! Is this a time for courtesy with pigs?"

'The Governess then ordered them to be killed, and God was served that all the good wine appeared too.'

Dona Isabel had important relations in the city. They wer immediately informed of her arrival and they had the good sens to take out a crew of seamen, clothed in gaily-coloured silks, t work the death-ship into harbour. On the quay they were me with banners flying, soldiers under arms, and a salute of artillery "All who came on board the ship," notes Quiros, "having see how little there was, wondered she should ever have arrived i safety, and praised God she should have been spared." We hor they praised him too.

They arrived at Manila on February 11, 1596, having le Peru the previous April. Next year the Governess returned Peru, having buried one husband and married another. Strang to say, Quiros was again her pilot. After another voyage "incredible hardships and troubles," they reached Acapulc "There I, Captain Pedro Fernandez de Quiros, took leave of th Governess and embarked on board a passenger ship for Peru —with what relief he leaves us to imagine.

AUSTRIALIA AND AUSTRALIA

UNDETERRED by the appalling experiences on his first voyage
cross the South Sea, Quiros returned to Peru determined to
resume his explorations at the first opportunity. He was convinced that the many islands recently discovered in the south-
west Pacific gave evidence of a continent in that region in just
the same way as Columbus' voyages to the West Indies had
preceded his discovery of the mainland. We can imagine him
asking the authorities the pertinent question, where would they
have been if Columbus had been prevented from sailing a
second time?

His arguments carried little weight with the Viceroy or at the
Court of Madrid, whither he returned in 1600. That was a
Holy Year, so he started off on a pilgrimage to Rome in pilgrim's
habit, staff in hand. Here he was well entertained by the
Spanish Ambassador, who invited all the leading mathematicians,
astrologers, cosmographers and pseudo-scientists to meet him
and examine him. They were properly impressed by his knowledge, particularly by what he told them about magnetic varia-
tion. At the Papal Court, too, he was favourably received, and
Clement VIII gave him letters to the King of Spain urging him
to continue the explorations so auspiciously begun.

This pilgrimage marks the turning point in Quiros' life. He
had always been a notably pious and loyal individual; he may
well have felt that the successful outcome of his last voyage was
due to a miraculous intervention of Providence on his behalf, so
unlikely had it seemed that they would ever reach land in safety.
The sight of the Papal City in all its jubilee grandeur, the bless-
ing bestowed upon him by the Holy Father himself, the gift of
a piece of the True Cross (obtained with some difficulty), were
enough to turn anyone's head. Henceforward Quiros became
a man with a fixed idea; to discover the great Southland, to

bring salvation to the millions of lost souls who must inhabit it
Riches and power were never his aim. His was the holy en
thusiasm of the missionary explorer. And the conviction tha
he died on the point of achieving his high aim was strong
enough to win the support of leading geographers even in th
Age of Reason. It was the claim made by Quiros, supported b
Alexander Dalrymple in England and the President de Brosses in
France, which sent Cook and Bougainville upon their voyages.

Quiros returned from Rome to Madrid in 1602. In spite o
the Papal letters he carried, his reception was still cool. Th
King's advisers pointed out that after a long war with Englan
the treasury was not in a position to waste money on anothe
wild-goose chase. An enthusiast like Quiros was not so easil
put off. He continued to bombard the Council of State and th
Council of the Indies with petitions, until he obtained throug
the former an order to the Viceroy of Peru to fit out two ship
at His Majesty's expense to explore "New Guinea, Java Majo
and other southern lands and islands, returning by that part o
the world to these My kingdoms in Spain." These instruction
were strengthened by recommendations showing the hig
opinion held of Quiros at Rome: "a worker, quiet, disinterested
of decent life, zealous for the service of God and for My service
The mathematicians at Rome affirm that there are few pilot
who know so much as he does."

It had taken him five years to get that testimonial, but h
was not yet at the end of his quest. He reached Lisbon to
late to catch the annual *flota* to the New World. The vessel in
which he secured a passage was wrecked on the farther side o
the Atlantic. He arrived at Lima without a penny in hi
pocket, encumbered by two small orphan nephews which h
had characteristically picked up on the way. There was n
room for them at any inn, nor had he money to pay for a lodg
ing. A few days after his arrival the house from which he wa
watching a procession collapsed and he retired to hospital with
a broken arm; worse still, the Governess was on his tracks
and her second husband was doing his best to dissuade the
Viceroy from paying any attention to him.

But royal orders had to be obeyed and ultimately three small
ships were made ready for him—one of 150 tons, another of 120
(Quiros' estimates) and a pinnace or *zabra*. He named the
Capitana, S. Pedro y S. Paulo, the *Almiranta, S. Pedrico*, and
the pinnace, *Los Tres Reyes*. His crew included 300 men, six
Franciscans and four friars of the Order of St. John to tend the
sick; learning from past experience, he took no women with
him. In command of the *Almiranta* he placed Luis Vaez de
Torres, a Portuguese about whom little was known, but whose
discoveries on this voyage entitle him to be called the last of
the great line of Portuguese pilots: Diaz, Da Gama, Magellan
and Quiros himself. Quiros' particular friend and admirer was
his young secretary, Luis de Belmonte Bermudez, who was
something of a poet and who supported Quiros when all the
others reviled him. Among the latter were Don Diego de
Prado y Tovar, the captain of the *Capitana*, an aristocrat who
despised Quiros as a "lunatic" and a Portuguese upstart; and
the Chief Pilot, Juan Ochoa de Bilboa, "foisted on me against
my will," who had recently been condemned to six years in the
galleys, but whose sentence was commuted on the understanding
that he would sail as pilot without pay. He proved to be a
quarrelsome shipmate and an astonishingly inefficient navigator.

The ships were well stocked for a long voyage when they
sailed from Callao in December 1605. In addition to the usual
provisions, Quiros took what is probably the earliest apparatus
for distilling fresh water of which there is any description: "A
brick oven to be built over one of the hearths in order to make
sweet water from sea water, with a copper instrument he had
with him." Further details about the "instrument" are lacking, but we are told that it provided two or three jars of drinking
water a day.

With all his difficulties behind him, Quiros determined to
make the day of sailing a memorable occasion. He dressed
himself and all his officers in the habit of friars (one can imagine
how Don Diego loathed all this fancy dress business). As the
royal standard was unfurled, every man in the crew fell to his
knees to pray Our Lady of Loreto (whose shrine Quiros had

visited) to send them success. All the artillery and musketr
in the ships was shot off, and every vessel in the harbour salute
their enormous banners as they were displayed—"white an
blue, all full of waves, with a red cross in the middle and a scro
with *En Solo Dios Va Puesta Mi Esperanza* in white letter
. . . the royal standard in crimson damask with a golden fring
. . . the image of the Virgin of Loreto . . . the Prince of th
Apostles. . . ." As one of the crew wrote, "With our good wi
and desire to serve God and spread our Holy Catholic Faith
and aggrandize the royal crown of the King our Lord, all seeme
easy to us."

As soon as they were at sea Quiros issued minute instruction
for the guidance of his subordinates. They are typical of "tha
talker," as Prado calls him: high-flown, verbose, pettifogging
but at the same time sensible and humane in what appertaine
to the discipline of the crew and their behaviour towards natives
There was to be no swearing, no gambling (backgammon board
were to be thrown overboard), no blaspheming; daily service
were to be attended by all; everyone was to respect the person
and property of natives, behaving to them "as fathers to chil
dren." The course to be sailed was W.S.W. to 30° S. If no lanc
was discovered by then, the ships were to turn N.W. to 10° 15′ S
If they still had not sighted land, course was to be set for Santa
Cruz, the position of which was set down at 1850 leagues from
Callao.

By January 22 they were in 26° S., but the initial enthusiasm
had cooled. Quiros himself fell ill soon after the start. De-
spondent questions were already being asked: "Whither are
they taking us, in this great gulf, in the winter season?" It
was then that he made a fatal mistake. "We were obliged, by
the force of winds and sea, to stand on a W.N.W. course." So
Quiros; but the others add more. Torres strongly objected,
wishing to continue to 30° S. as originally intended. Prado
was convinced (on the evidence of a cloudbank) that they were
just on the point of great discoveries when Quiros turned N.W.
at the instigation of his crew, who wished to take the ship to
the Philippines. When he remonstrated he was told curtly

hat he (Quiros) "knew what he was doing. . . . From thenceforward he took the greatest dislike and illwill towards me and
said to one of his friends that he would leave me ashore on a
desert island."

On their new course they reached Anaa, somewhat north-east
of Tahiti, with which early historians confused it. The natives
were friendly and willingly replenished their stock of provisions.
It was in this island that they set up a wooden cross which was
found by the commander of the Spanish frigate *Aquila* when he
rediscovered the island in 1774.

Thence they continued west in the direction of Santa Cruz.
For many weeks the three ships sailed without sight of land,
their wakes making long white tracks through the lonely seas.
The men demanded cards and dice, and when Quiros persisted
in his Sunday School attitude, murmurings and quarrels begot
of boredom disturbed the quiet of the long summer days beneath
a blazing sun. The Chief Pilot had to be disarmed after wound-
ing a man. Quiros was a sick man and even more ineffective
as a leader than usual; who but he, at this stage of the voyage,
would have nailed the following notice to the mainmast—

"No person shall take the name of God in vain, on pain of
a fine of one dollar, for the souls."

Fines in the middle of the South Sea proving ineffective, he
found himself regretting that he had not brought irons with
him from Peru. In the mood of high idealism in which he
sailed he appears to have imagined that, as he regarded this as
a holy voyage, everyone on board would naturally behave like
a saint.

As there was still no sign of the promised island he summoned
a council of pilots. He estimated the distance to Santa Cruz as
1850 leagues. The Chief Pilot claimed that by dead reckoning
they had already sailed 2300, but an examination of his calculations showed an error of at least 600 leagues. As a matter of
fact when, two days later, they sighted Taumaco, 60 leagues east
of Santa Cruz, Torres reckoned the distance as 1940, and the
new pilot at 1750—striking evidence of the accuracy of Quiros'

original calculations. In consequence of Bilboa's proved incompetence, as well as of his insubordinate character, he was disrated in favour of de Leza and sent on board the *Almiranta* under arrest. "Presently it was reported to the Captain that the ship was in a state of mutiny owing to what he had said in public." "Is there anyone who objects that I send the Chief Pilot out of the ship?" asked Quiros. "One who spoke in his favour was ordered to hold his tongue, being told that the day before he had just said the contrary."

This was probably Prado who, now that land was in sight, behaved in a very odd manner for one who was supposed to be the senior officer. He says that he informed Quiros by means of the confessional about an incipient mutiny, apparently not venturing to tell him to his face. Odder still is his account of what followed: "The said Don Diego knew who were the mutineers and how they wanted him for a head, but he did not want to mix in such conflicts and lose the honour which he had gained in his Majesty's service, so he at once shifted his things to the *Almiranta*, whereat the Captain thereof (Torres) was very pleased. The next day the surgeon did the same"—in fact they preserved their "honour" by deserting their chief at the moment when they should have been supporting his authority. He goes on to say that Torres told him that Quiros intended to have the Chief Pilot garrotted and thrown into the sea. Yet Torres states that when he demanded severe punishment for Bilboa, Quiros refused to do more than arrest him. In view of what Quiros himself had told the Governess to do in similar circumstances, his weak handling of the situation is all the more curious. Some ambiguous notes which he afterwards wrote on the subject of discipline show that by this date religious mania had got the better of his common sense: "He said that justice was an excellent virtue, and very necessary in the world; but yet let it be exercised by others who have the habit, rather than by him among those who use but little reason, the witnesses (e.g. Prado) being enemies."

Anyhow the discovery of the charming island of Taumaco in the Duff group extricated him from a potentially dangerous situation. The inhabitants were hospitable and informative; as for their chief, Tumai, "never was there a barbarian who possessed the good sense of this one." He knew all about their previous visit to the neighbouring Santa Cruz, only he begged them to use their arquebuses on his enemies, not his friends. The islanders seemed astonishingly well informed about events in other islands and the geography of the region, as well they might be, to judge from the astonishing system of traffic and exchange among the neighbouring Trobriand islanders, described by Malinowski in his *Argonauts of the Western Pacific*. Indeed, in this book may be found not only the best description of contemporary Pacific craft, but a possible explanation of the reason why nearly all early travellers were welcomed so generously and why that welcome so soon turned to blows. Being ignorant of native customs, they did not understand the natives' attitude to the giving and receiving of presents. When gifts of food were not made with the regularity they expected, they failed to see that the fault lay in themselves, in so far as their own generosity did not measure up to the natives' expectation.

Prado, too, describes the magnificent sixty-foot canoes in which the Polynesians made their incredible voyages. They carried as much sail as the Spanish vessels, though he notes that they can only sail before the wind. Besides a sail deck, they had a sort of covered platform for stores, the water being carried in hollow canes, each tube holding four gallons. As they were of shallow draft they were easily steered by two great stern oars. Every explorer has been impressed by the size, speed and variety of such craft—double canoes, dugouts, with outriggers on one or both sides to give them stability, single canoes which shoot like fish through the water, and great war canoes manned by 60 or 80 men. In craft such as these, still fashioned with stone tools and still navigated by traditional knowledge of weather and stars, the Polynesians had colonised the Pacific before 1000 A.D.

Tumai provisioned them generously and told them what they could find to the south—60 islands and (opening his arms wide) "a very great land, which he called Manicolo." To explain the distance he pointed to the sun, laid his head on his hand, shut his eyes and with his fingers counted the number of nights the voyage lasted. The continent, thought Quiros, lay just where he expected. Without delay the ships sped south, though it is to be regretted that Tumai's kindness was repaid by kidnapping four of his subjects to act as interpreters. There was no longer need to be particular about the course—"Put the ships' heads where they like, for God will guide them as may be right," he cried.

In this ecstasy of religious enthusiasm Quiros soon found his reward. On May 20, 1606, after passing a succession of islands, they anchored in the widest bay in the South Sea, a bay "big enough for all the fleets in the world." He named it the Bay of St. Philip and St. James, and the new-found-land, with a delicate compliment to Philip III, who was also Archduke of Austria, Austrialia del Espiritu Santo. To Quiros it seemed the climax of his life's endeavour, the continent so long desired. Everywhere to the southward there was evidence of land. Actually, what he saw was the foreshortened line of the mountains of the New Hebrides which, we are told by those who have seen them from the angle their discoverer saw them, do indeed look like a mainland, the successive island ranges overlapping each other for hundreds of miles away to the south.

On such an occasion it was only fit that the landing should be made with due ceremony. Torres' advance party had an unsatisfactory brush with the inhabitants; that must be overlooked. On the eve of Whitsunday Quiros made a speech from the poop announcing the creation of a new Order of his own devising, the Order of the Knights of the Holy Ghost. To each man, even the black drummer, he handed the insignia of his Order, a blue cross to be worn over a robe of blue taffeta. Cynics like Prado might snigger over these "absurdities," but the man's blazing sincerity certainly impressed the crew. "Gentlemen," he announced with emotion, "this is the eve of my long desired day": let each man confess himself and tomorrow let us dedicate the land. As darkness fell, rockets exploded into the sky, fire-wheels and lanterns lit up the banners floating aloft, drums sounded, all the bells in the ships were rung, and every gun was fired till the echoes pealed across the bay and they could hear the answering shouts of the natives from the shore.

On Whitsunday the formal landing was made, with the Royal Ensign and all the banners proudly displayed. Stepping ashore, Quiros knelt down in thanksgiving—"To God alone be the honour and the glory!" Then, kissing the ground, "O Land! Sought for so long, intended to be found by many, and so desired of me!" The friars knelt as the Cross was erected and Quiros took possession of the land, together with all seas and lands to the uttermost pole, in the name of the Holy Trinity, the Catholic Church, St. Francis and his Order, St. John and his Order, in the name of the Order of the Holy Spirit and in the name of His Majesty.

The colony was to be called the New Jerusalem; the town, Vera Cruz; the near-by stream, Jordan. Of course, the first building, hastily constructed of boughs and leaves, was a church. On that site, he declared, there would arise a church greater than that of St. Peter's at Rome. The officials of a Municipality were announced; his friend Belmonte being one of the magistrates, Torres Master of the Camp, and Don Diego de Prado relegated to the position of Store Keeper General. The latter's comment on the whole proceeding is not surprising: "it was all wind." Never for a moment did he believe this was *Terra Australis*. "We have only found black devils with poisoned arrows," he pointed out to Quiros with some relish; "what has become of the riches? We quite understand that all your affairs are imaginary and as such have gone off in wind." Bilboa naturally tried to take advantage of Quiros' excitement by pleading to be forgiven. But even when the plea was supported by a friar, and though he freed two slaves to mark the occasion, Quiros refused to pardon him. Personal injuries he could forget, but inasmuch as the King's service had been slighted no pardon was possible.

A few days later the feast of Corpus Christi was celebrated in holy exultation with all the traditional pomp of Spain. The natives, peering through the undergrowth, may well have been impressed by the chanting, the vestments, the incense, the ringing of · bells. Nevertheless a shower of poisoned arrows greeted any party which penetrated the hinterland and the sound of distant war drums disturbed the camp every night. Quiros made light of such matters in the rosy pictures he later painted of the land. "I am able to say with good reason, that a land more delightful, healthy and fertile; a site better supplied with quarries, timber, clay for tiles, bricks for founding a great city . . . could not be found. No port could be found more agreeable . . . nor is there any other land that could sustain many strangers so pleasantly, if what has been written is well considered. . . . I have never seen nor have heard of such advantages." In later years its attractions grew in retrospect till there was born that definitive myth of the Great Southland which convinced so many geographers for such an astonishing length of time.

At the first opportunity he tried to explore the coastline and see what lay behind the mountains in the distance. On June 8 the ships put to sea, taking with them some native boys they had captured. As the land receded one of them begged pitifully to be put ashore. "Silence, child," replied Quiros, "you know not what you ask. Greater good awaits you than the sight and communion with heathen parents and friends."

What happened during the next three days is a problem which cannot be unravelled at this date. All the witnesses agree that as soon as the bay was cleared the weather became threatening, and Quiros tried to regain port with a view to settling there for the winter. On the night of June 11 they tried to anchor in the bay, but could find no bottom (nor could Captain Cook when he visited the island in 1774). In the middle of the night, according to Quiros and his pilot, the lights of the *Almiranta* disappeared and next morning their own ship was found to be out of sight of land with a gale blowing from the south. After striving in vain to beat back, Quiros put the helm about and sped north towards Santa Cruz. On the other hand, Torres says that he was deserted by the *Capitana*, which "departed at one hour past midnight without any notice given to us, and without making any signal." Prado, on the suspect evidence of his own prejudice and what was later told him by some of Quiros' sailors, states definitely that the crew of the *Capitana* mutinied. He quotes them as saying that they were driven out to sea while Quiros was asleep. "He came out at mid-day, as usual from his stern cabin and asked why they had not anchored behind the cape; in reply he was told to shut his mouth and go to his cabin, where they put the Portuguese grocer and his nephews with guards; and they ordered the jars of wine belonging to the Portuguese to be brought out and divided among the sailors." If that was the case, it is difficult to see how the ship could ever have reached Mexico in safety, with only one death to be recorded.

As his ship drove north Quiros describes himself as following the advice of his officers to return to New Spain. His original orders were to return on June 21 in any case, and now there was no time to spare to attempt a dead beat back to Santo. Still under the impression that he had discovered a continent, it was supremely important that he should return with the news as quickly as possible. Torres could be left to continue the work of exploration, acting on the instructions left with him.

As the wind would not serve for Manila, the *Capitana* continued north until she was in latitude 38° N., where she turned east along the normal route of returning galleons. During the long voyage home Quiros made an incoherent will, which shows the extent to which the idealist had by this time lost contact with reality. "In these regions which it has been the will of God to show me," he desired that "no falcons or other birds of prey," such as had despoiled the Indies, should be allowed to enter. "It is money, I say, that they want and more money, though it be torn from men's entrails." From the incomprehensible verbiage of this strange document the one point that stands out clearly is the author's consideration for the lives and souls of those heathen islanders which providence had delivered into the hands of his countrymen. He knew too well how, even with the best of them, it was a case of first falling on their knees and then on the aborigines. But if he was in the habit of speaking as wildly as he wrote we cannot wonder that he was treated on his return to Mexico in October 1606 as "a fool and a madman."

There are many gaps in our knowledge of the early history of Australia and of the obscure sea captains who first fell in with its western coast, more often than not by accident. Almost every seafaring nation can lay a claim of some sort to its dis-covery: it all depends on what is meant by the word "dis-covery." The first sight of a new country? Its recognition? Or its effective colonisation?

The Spanish claim has recently been strengthened, at least as regards the first of these interpretations, by the discovery in a bundle of MSS. offered for sale a few years ago of the " Relacion" of Don Diego de Prado. Before its publication in 1929 the only first-hand description of the strait between New Guinea and Australia discovered by Torres after he left Santo was the latter's official letter sent from Manila in July 1607. So anxious were the Spanish authorities lest this discovery of first-rate import-ance should become known to the Dutch and English heretics already roaming those seas that the letter remained hidden until Alexander Dalrymple, a clerk in the East India Company, dis-covered a copy at some indeterminate date towards the end of the eighteenth century (see below, p. 171). Dalrymple gave his copy of the letter to Burney, who published it in the second volume of his *History of the Discoveries in the South Seas* in 1803, and was the first to advance the claim that Torres dis-covered "The Great Terra Australis," by which he meant Australia. It is not yet certain where the original is to be found, though Quiros certainly knew of its contents when he was in Madrid in 1608.

Such is the story, unique in the history of exploration, of the records concerning the discovery of the Torres Strait and also as it appears, of Australia. Originally discovered in 1606, no one knew of the existence of the strait until a century and a half later, and no one sailed through it again until Cook did so in 1770. The third European to sail through it was Captain Bligh when, in 1789, he made his amazing open boat journey after the mutiny on board the *Bounty* over two thousand miles away to the eastward.

To return to the story of its discovery. After awaiting the return of the *Capitana* for fifteen days, Torres opened the Viceroy's sealed orders to find out what he was to do next. It was somewhat humiliating to find that Prado was to take command in the event of anything happening to Quiros, for Torres had so far played a bigger part in the voyage than had this disgruntled gentleman. However, Prado had the sense to leave all navigational questions to Torres, whom he appointed Chief Pilot. Their instructions ordered them to continue the search for the southern continent as far as 20° S., then to return to Manila via the north coast of New Guinea. Torres was anxious to carry out these orders, though the opinion of Prado and the majority seems to have been against him. At all events, having found that Santo, as it is usually called today, was after all an island, they sailed south-west as far as 21° S., where the condition of the ship and the state of the weather forced them to turn north-west into the Coral Sea. Thereby they missed the opportunity of discovering the eastern coast of Australia.

They were prevented by contrary winds from weathering the eastern point of New Guinea, as they had intended, and were forced instead to follow its southern coastline. As a result they made the most important discovery of the whole voyage. After passing the site of the modern Port Moresby, they followed the coast of the Gulf of Papua as it trended round to the south-west. Here they were in the most dangerous waters in the world—shark-infested, and bristling with half-submerged reefs which compose the northern end of the Great Barrier Reef. Only miraculous luck and the shallow draft of their little vessel saved them from catastrophe. For two months they fought with heat and flies, reefs, shoals and currents for a distance of 300 leagues, until they found the coast of New Guinea turning north-west again and they followed it up into the comparative safety of the Moluccas.

In this way they discovered what Dalrymple was the first to call Torres Strait. The few bare sentences in which Torres

describes the event, the full importance of which he did not
realise, because he knew nothing of the existence of Australia,
mentions latitudes which have given rise to some controversy.
Even in Prado's fuller account, the language is so vague as to
make their exact course uncertain. It seems that they went as
far south as 11°, which is farther south than the tip of Cape York
peninsula. Before turning north again Prado says that on
October 3 they saw "other islands towards the north and among
them one bigger than the rest"—probably Prince of Wales in
10° 46', or Thursday Island. Torres adds: "We had to go out
(of the Gulf of Papua) turning south-west in the said depth, to
11°, and the bank (the Barrier Reef) goes lower: there were
very large islands and they seemed more on the southern part:
they were inhabited by very corpulent black people, naked."
If "the southern part" means Cape York, the passage they sailed
through was not Torres Strait, strictly so called, which lies
between New Guinea and the islands, but Endeavour Passage,
which lies between Prince of Wales Island and the peninsula.

If Columbus may be said to have discovered America in
1492, when he sighted a West India island which he thought
to be Cipangu, so Torres and Prado may be said to have discovered Australia in 1606. There is, however, a possibility that
their discovery was anticipated by a few months by the Dutch.
The best evidence for this is a route map, showing land as far
south as 13°, which records the voyage of a certain Captain
Janszoon in the *Duyfken* to the Gulf of Carpentaria earlier that
same year. In any case the latter did not realise that a strait
existed between New Guinea and Australia, nor did anyone
else, save Torres, until the days of Cook.

As in the case of the Magellan Straits, the question arises,
did Torres know of the strait before he sailed through it? The
answer is, almost certainly not. In some of their maps Ortelius
and Mercator mark New Guinea as an island, but they explain
that the question is not settled. Wytfliet's Louvain map of 1597
marks it clearly, together with the Solomon Islands. But in all
these cases the strait is marked somewhere about 20° S., not
10°. The very conservative map by Molyneux published by

Hakluyt in 1599 shows no land at all to the south of New Guinea. A rarer map, which Torres could not possibly have seen because it was in the Royal Library at Windsor, is that by Jean Rotz of Dieppe, dated 1542. In this mysterious map the north coast of Australia is marked so clearly that many have accepted it as proof of an earlier discovery, possibly by the French or Portuguese. Other early maps of French or Portuguese origin chart this coast with remarkable accuracy.

The rest of the voyage was comparatively uneventful. They reached Manila in May 1607. There they parted company. What happened to Torres, no one knows. Prado turns up again at Goa in 1613, whence he sent home some accurate charts of the bay at Santo and parts of the south coast of New Guinea (which was not surveyed again until Admiral Moresby's expedition in 1873), together with two letters abusing Quiros as "an impostor and a lunatic," "a liar and a fraud," who is not to be trusted on any account. He returned overland via Ormuz and ended his days as a monk in the Order of St. Basil.

Quiros died at Panama in 1614 or 1615, we hope before he knew of this added abuse. The story of his last years is a sad one. He failed to impress the authorities of Peru with his grandiloquent description of his "new world." Back in Spain he besieged the Court for seven years with no more success. In the hundreds of memorials he wrote to press his case *Terra Australis* is painted in ever rosier colours, its size expands, its population multiplies, its resources are exaggerated. In area it becomes a quarter of the globe, a continent far greater than Europe and Asia Minor combined. In importance it exceeds all the Spanish Dominions beyond the seas. Its latitude offers a fairer climate than Spain. "Here may presently be built a very great and populous city, whose inhabitants will enjoy the above-mentioned commodities, as well as those which my small imagination is unable to set forth. . . . I do not exaggerate if I say that it can maintain and accommodate 200,000 Spaniards." He bids his royal master reflect what profit flowed from the discoveries of Columbus. From a native population which he somehow estimates at 30 million, a tribute of at least 20 million ducats could be extorted. Think what riches such a country could produce in a hundred years' time!

He sang the charms of his continent in vain. The old arguments were adduced; that the treasury could not afford more expeditions, that further discoveries would drain the dwindling man-power of the mother country. The suspicions entertained by the authorities about Quiros' fitness to lead another expedition were fortified by the accounts sent in by Torres and others, long before Prado's denunciations reached them. In the New World Mendaña's heirs provided more scandal, obviously inspired by the fear that if Quiros sailed again their claims to the Solomons would be endangered.

The members of the Royal Council were sufficiently acute to realise that a bare refusal was dangerous in the case of such an enthusiast as Quiros. Already some of his memorials had fallen into foreign hands, two being published in *Purchas hi Pilgrimes* and another by a Dutch editor. If they were no careful he would sell his information to a foreign power, a Columbus had been on the point of doing, and "this Pedr Fernandez de Quiros has got it into his head to be anothe Columbus." Seeing that he was grown "very discontente and suspicious," they recommended giving him "a well pai appointment at court, or where it may seem best."

The decision finally taken was peculiarly faithless to on who had served Spain so well. Quiros was to be promised th command of an expedition if he returned to Peru. At the sam time the Viceroy there was secretly advised to keep him quie with promises which were not to be honoured. Buoyed u with such empty hopes Quiros crossed the Atlantic for the las time, but he died before he reached Peru. With him, it ha been well said, died the naval heroism of Spain.

THE DUTCH VOYAGERS

BROADLY speaking, three periods may be distinguished in the history of the Pacific: the Spanish in the sixteenth century; the Dutch in the seventeenth; the English and French in the eighteenth.

"The Prodigious increase of the Netherlands in their Domestick and Foreign Trade, Riches, and multitude of Shipping, is the envy of the present, and may be the wonder of all future generations." The first half of the seventeenth century, the brief period beginning with their country's liberation from Spain and ending with its decline in the face of attacks by France and England, was indeed the golden age of Dutch seamen. For proof of their predominance in maritime affairs we need look no further than our own sea vocabulary. "Deck," "boom," "yacht," "sloop," "skipper," "cruiser," are all Dutch importations. Or walk up Charing Cross Road and see the maps of the Dutch cartographers, Plancius, Hondius or Blaeu, hanging in the windows. Indeed their fame has been such as to overshadow the really excellent work done by the English at the turn of the century. Topographical maps by Saxton and Speed (many of whose maps were engraved at Amsterdam) are in every house; but few appreciate the terrestrial and celestial globes of Emery Molyneux, or his extremely accurate world map engraved by Wright and published by Hakluyt in 1599—Shakespeare's 'New Map with the Augmentation of the Indies." Here one looks in vain for such figments of the imagination as *Terra Australis*, still to be found in most of the Dutch atlases.

Compared with their predecessors, the Dutch are dull fellows. They lack the vision of the first explorers. Their strictly commercial aims are seldom ennobled by the ideals which partially atone for the predatory instincts of the Spanish *conquistadores*: no Dutchman ever sailed *Ad maioram gloriam*

Dei. Their journals are sober statements of facts, though en
livened by lavish illustrations and beautiful maps. On the othe
hand, they were far better sailors. They did more than an
other people to improve the efficiency of the sailing ship. Bein
under the necessity of making longer voyages than their Spanis
rivals, they were forced to economise in the handling of thei
ships. No summer cruises for them: every voyage to th
Pacific or the Spice Islands meant going half-way round th
world. In various ways they so improved the technique o
sailing a ship that they were able to cut down the ratio of me
to tonnage, and this in turn enabled them to carry more carg
and provisions, to lower freights, and thus capture the carryin
trade. On Quiros' last expedition there were 300 men to 28
tons of shipping; on Schouten's voyage there were 87 men t
330 tons, and only three men died in a voyage right round th
world. Other commanders were not so fortunate, but there i
no doubt that their standards of diet and cleanliness were fa
superior to those of other nations.

During the last years of Elizabeth's reign there existed
friendly rivalry between Dutchmen and Englishmen for supre
macy in Eastern waters. When Philip of Spain prohibite
trade with the northern nations, the heretics naturally went t
get the spices themselves. During the last decade of th
century they pooled their knowledge and sailed in each other'
ships. Navigational manuals like *The Mariner's Mirror* o
The Haven-finding Art were translated from the Dutch
Hakluyt was responsible for the English edition of Linschoten'
itinerary to the east. John Davis of Dartmouth sailed as pilo
in a Dutch ship on his last voyage, when he was murdered b
Japanese pirates. They learnt from each other and vied wit
each other in finding out the best route to the Moluccas. Th
English quest for a North-West Passage having failed, th
Dutch continued the equally vain search for one in the north
east. Most captains preferred the Cape route, but others trie
the Magellan route for trade or privateering (the distinctio
between the two was equally vague for both nations).

In the end the Cape route won, and the East India Companie

of both nations settled down to a far more efficient exploitation of the riches of the Indies than the Portuguese had ever attempted. Then the English dropped out of the running, partly because no empire builder of the stature of the great Governors of the Dutch East India Company, like Coen or Van Diemen, made an appearance, partly because civil broils at home led to a general deterioration in our efficiency at sea. From the date of the "massacre" of Amboyna in 1623 (a small affair by twentieth-century standards) our attention was diverted from the East Indies to India itself. What at the time looked like a confession of failure, proved in the end a far greater prize.

Of the feelers put out by the Dutch to find the best way to the Moluccas, only the Pacific voyages concern us here. In 1598 opinion was still uncertain about the advantages of the Cape route, so two expeditions were equipped by private enterprise to try the possibilities of the Pacific. The first to leave Rotterdam consisted of five ships under the command of Jacob Mahu, who "died of a flux" early in the voyage, to be succeeded in command by De Cordes. Their orders were to circumnavigate the globe and sell a cargo of woollen cloth on the way. It is typical of the period that the chief pilot was an Englishman, William Adams.

Off South America, the ships scattered, and not one succeeded in rounding the globe. Adams' ship reached Japan with only 24 survivors, and "only 5 men of us able to goe." He made such a good impression on the "Japanners" that the Mikado refused to let him leave the island, though he managed to write some letters home. Before he died at an advanced age, he initiated the savages into the art of shipbuilding, and founded the Dutch trade with Japan which, in spite of periodical massacres, lasted longer than that of any other nation.

Of the other ships, one reached the Moluccas, where it was seized by the Portuguese. Another, under Dirck Gerritsz, was blown to 64° S. after issuing from the Straits of Magellan. He sighted what we call the South Shetlands, but what he thought were the snowy peaks of "the great Zuidland." He was captured by the Spaniards. Still another, under Sebald de Weert,

lost heart and returned via the Falklands. Not knowing that
they had twice previously been sighted by Elizabethan explorers,
John Davis and Richard Hawkins (who named them "Hawkins-
Maidenland as a perpetual memory of her Chastity and my
endeavour"), he claimed them as a new discovery under the
name of the Sebaldines.

On his return east through the Straits, he passed the second
expedition of 1598 on its way west. De Noort, its commander,
started life as an innkeeper, but, says an old writer, "he had a
strong passion for glory," and he certainly proved more fortunate
than his rivals. He picked up another English pilot at Plymouth, together with an odd character, "John Calleway, of
London, a musician and player on instruments." De Noort
circumnavigated the world on the lines laid down by Drake.
He plundered successfully up the coast, and fought an action
with a Spanish squadron from Manila under the command of
Antonio De Morga, lawyer, historian, Lieutenant-Governor
turned Admiral for the occasion. Though one may excuse De
Noort's comparative ill-success in the fight on the score that his
men were fewer and more exhausted by their long voyage than
their enemies, one cannot excuse his cruelties to the Fuegian
Indians, or his lack of originality with respect to the route he
took. However, he did succeed in being the first Dutchman
to sail round the world, though only nine men out of 248
returned alive.

Thus only one ship out of the nine which set out in 1598
ever returned to Holland.

Undeterred by these terrible losses, another squadron set
forth in 1614 under Joris Spilbergen (or Spielbergen), a gallant
and experienced East India commander. As his mission was
primarily plunder, no fresh discoveries were made, the usual
northern route across the ocean being followed; but in consequence of its semi-official character, it was better managed and
far more successful in fighting capacity than its predecessors.
Five out of the six ships which set out—*Great Sun*, *Full Moon*,
Huntsman, *Aeolus*, *Sea Mew*, *Morning Star*—succeeded in
making the second Dutch circumnavigation, a higher proportion

han in any previous voyage. A Spanish squadron was soundly
eaten off Callao and three of the enemy's ships were sunk. In
616 he reached Java, where he met a rival expedition which
had sailed under private enterprise a few months after him and
had made far more important discoveries. Accounts of both
expeditions were published together in a lavishly illustrated
book entitled *The East and West Indian Mirror,* which appeared
in 1619. (See illustration, p. 27.)

The promoter of the latter expedition was Isaac Le Maire,
an old merchant living at Hoorn, surrounded by twenty-two
children. He and his fellow burghers sturdily opposed the
monopolistic tendencies of the Dutch East India Company. In
the face of powerful opposition, he obtained a charter for a
Southern or Australian Company to trade in Tartary, Japan,
"the great Zuidland" and its surrounding seas. Unfortunately
for his "project," as the Elizabethans would have called it, the
charter of his rivals gave them control of all known entrances
to these seas, both by the Cape and the Straits of Magellan. But
what if there was another entrance? In many of the maps of
Drake's voyage, particularly that by Hondius, Tierra del Fuego
is shown as an island. If it were possible to sail round this island
and avoid using the straits he would be able to trick his opponents
out of their restriction of what he regarded as legitimate enterprise. An East India pilot named Willem Schouten agreed
with him, and offered to share the cost. It was arranged that
Schouten should sail as Master Mariner or Patron, the office of
Merchant and President being filled by Isaac's son, Jacob.
Besides being the first to start the series of ill-starred South Sea
Companies, Le Maire's aim differed from all previous Dutch
voyagers in that the principal object was not plunder, still less
a new route to the Moluccas, but a definite search for the land
described by Quiros in the memorial which had found its way
into Dutch hands. The fears entertained by the Spanish authorities about Quiros' loquacity were now to be substantiated.

"A big ship and a yacht," the *Eendracht* and the *Hoorn,*
sailed from the Texel in June 1615. The *Hoorn* was almost the
same tonnage as Magellan's *Victoria,* but her consort was twice

the size.   For rations, exclusive of meat and fish, they we:
allowed

> One can of beer per day
> 4 lbs. biscuit per man per week
> $\frac{1}{2}$ lb. butter and $\frac{1}{2}$ lb. suet per man per week.

As before, an Englishman, this time a carpenter, was taken o
at Plymouth.   Instead of making straight for the coast of Sout
America, a call was made at Sierra Leone, where a few bea
and some cheap Nuremberg knives were exchanged for 25,00
lemons. Whether the deal was made by chance, or as the resu
of a knowledge of the causes of scurvy, it is impossible to say; bu
there can be no doubt that this was the chief reason why on
two men died during the rest of their fifteen months' voyage.

Like everyone else, they careened at Port Desire befor
entering the Pacific, and, like everyone else, they found evid
ence of giants in the land now usually called *Terra Gigantiur*
—this time an eleven-foot skeleton under a heap of stone
Unfortunately they lost the *Hoorn* here.   While breaming he
(another Dutch term, meaning to singe the weed off the botton
with burning furze), her pitch caught fire and she was burne
to the water's edge.

After sighting the Sebaldines, as they called them, they hel
on resolutely, leaving Cape Virgins twenty leagues to starboar
in their endeavour to see if Tierra del Fuego was really an island
On January 24, 1616, they found themselves in a narrow strait
eight leagues wide, with high land on either side.   That to th
east, white with snow and very perilous-looking, they calle
Staten Land, imagining it to be part of the great Southland
The new strait was named after the family of the leader an
promoter of the expedition, though Schouten later contested th
honour by claiming that he himself had made the discovery
Soon after, as they turned south-west into "very blue water,"
in which they saw whales by thousands, they began to battl
with the mountainous rollers which are formed by the great
Antarctic Drift being compressed into the 600-mile gap known
as Drake Strait, between America and the polar regions.   Here

Plate III

THE DISCOVERY OF CAPE HORN

Blaeu map *c.* 1618, showing route of Le Maire

Plate IV

WILLIAM DAMPIER

Portrait by T. Murray

hey saw what Drake probably never saw—the massive black
liffs of Cape Horn. They called it Hoorn, after their native
own, but to our minds, coloured by a thousand stories of hard-
hips suffered in that passage, the shortened form of Horn aptly
ymbolises the huge black tooth which terminates the continent.
Like many another crew, they were "russelled mightily by a
evere storm out of the south-west." As the first "willjewaws,"
or lashing squalls of sleet, struck them, and the ship began to
pitch in enormous hollow seas and deep troughed swells, they
hastened to stow their cannon in the waist, battened down the
hatches, and made everything fast. Four men in stout leather
erkins manned the tiller to keep her head into the wind. In
such weather no one can blame them for being a hundred miles
out in their longitude, with the consequence that academic
geographers at home showed a very inaccurate picture of the
new coastline. A section of a rare Blaeu map of 1618, here
reproduced, shows their route, and the giants they met on the
coast of Patagonia.

Gradually the storm subsided. They were able to master the
swift current that threatened to carry them back into the
Atlantic, and to climb out of these high latitudes, setting a
course for Juan Fernandez. Their object was *Terra Australis*,
but wind and sea forced them to follow a more northerly route
than they had originally intended. None the less, they succeeded in crossing the ocean in a more southerly latitude than
that of any previous voyager. The inaccuracy of their reckon-
ings makes it impossible to define many of the smaller islands
which they discovered in consequence, but it seems certain that
they passed through the southern part of the Low or Tuamotu
Archipelago in 15° S., south of the paradisal Society group, to
reach Hoorn Island between Samoa and Fiji, almost on the date
line. Le Maire sneered at Schouten for thinking this was part
of *Terra Australis*, but he himself confused it with one of the
Solomons.

They met with such a hospitable reception at this tiny island
that "we got to be as free and easy there as if we had been at
home." For once there was no fighting, probably because the

local chief took it upon himself to maintain discipline. Time
passed as in the Golden Age, eating hogs and game and coconuts
The illustrations to the narrative preserve for us the fantasti
spectacle of these solid Dutchmen, in broad-brimmed hats an
baggy trousers, entertaining the chief and his naked wives i
the moonlight with a dance to the accompaniment of the drum
and trumpets of the ship's band. They refused only one deli
cacy: the popular South Sea drink called kava, a potent i
pleasant drug which is made by chewing a type of pepper plan
and spitting the well-masticated pulp into a bowl. With th
best will in the world the visitors could not bring themselve
to drink it: "they had more than enough at the sight of it."

Underlying their hospitality there was always a suspicior
of the white men on the part of these well-mannered natives
Their relief at the prospect of the departure of the visitors i
illustrated by an incident which took place at the farewel
banquet held on board. "As we sat at table we showed then
that we intended to depart in two days' time, whereat the young
prince was so glad that he immediately jumped up from th
table and went into the gallery shouting out that we intendec
to depart in two days' time."

The only mistake of the voyage was made soon after leaving
Hoorn. Dalrymple, the eighteenth-century historian who wor-
shipped the name of Quiros, blames Schouten for doubting the
truth of his hero's claims, a scepticism "which is the natura
conclusion of a little ignorant mind." This may well have beer
the case, for when a council was held to determine their future
course, Le Maire, having "no doubt that *Terra Australis* wa
very near," was all for continuing due west. But Schouten won
the day by pointing out the dangers of falling in with the unknown coast of New Guinea if they did so. He advised stretching away to the north-north-west to sail round the north of it,
since at that date no one knew of a passage to the south. Evidently Schouten had lost his nerve for exploration, and Le Maire
had to comply with his professional advice. In consequence they
missed the larger Solomons altogether, though they discovered
and named the most northerly one of the group, Green Island.

hence they skirted the coast of New Ireland (which they took
o be New Guinea) and found themselves among the twenty-
ive islets now called the Admiralty Islands. Somewhat farther
vest Schouten Island testifies to their route.

In September 1616 they reached Java, where they found
pilbergen, who had arrived the previous March. Before they
eft home men had scoffed at them as "the gold seekers." Now
pilbergen and his men sneered at their failure to report any-
hing profitable, "although they pretended that they had dis-
overed a passage shorter than the usual one, which is very
mprobable, inasmuch as it took them fifteen months and three
lays to make the voyage to Ternate, though with a single ship."
Worse still was the behaviour of that hard man, Governor Coen,
vho confiscated their ship and sent them home in the charge of
Spilbergen for having infringed the monopoly of the Company.
[t was a singularly ungenerous recompense for so original a
voyage. Jacob Le Maire died on his way home, according to his
father on account of the "affront put upon him." Old Isaac's
pugnacity was once again aroused when Schouten returned to
tell the tale. He sued the Company for the cost of the ship, and
after two years' litigation won his case. Thus the existence of
the Strait of Le Maire was officially admitted as a consequence
of an action at law.

Not that this was necessary, for as soon as a report of the
supposed discovery reached the ears of the King of Spain, two
naval officers, the brothers Nodal, were sent out to settle the
question. They confirmed the report by sailing right round
Tierra del Fuego and back through the Straits of Magellan. In
addition they made their own contribution to geographical
knowledge by discovering the most southerly of all islands, the
lonely Diego Ramirez group, which they named after the distinguished cosmographer who sailed with them.

Animated by a hereditary hatred of the Spanish, Prince
Maurice of Nassau was an indefatigable patron of such enterprises as we have just described. In 1623, in order to "humble
the Spaniards by distressing them in their tenderest parts," he
equipped a fleet under Admiral L'Heremite for another raid in

the South Seas. This, the Nassau Fleet of 11 vessels and 1637
men, was the largest expedition ever sent out, but it met with
very moderate success considering its size. The admiral died
off Peru; their plunder was not impressive; their report of yet
another glimpse of the elusive continent between the straits
and Juan Fernandez has proved illusory, though it found its way
on to many maps. Only one ship of the original eleven succeeded in circumnavigating the world.

To make up for the poor showing of this fleet, Maurice sent
another under Captain Hendrick Brouwer in 1642. It was
equally fruitless, save for their accidental discovery that Staten
Land was really an island and not part of *Terra Australis*, the
confines of which at that date expand and retract like visions
in water. Brouwer died off the coast of Chile and his ships
returned via Cape Horn, the first to make the famous wool-
clipper passage from west to east.

At this stage of our story we must turn to the one voyage
which differs from all the others hitherto recounted in this
book, in so far as that it was not from east to west. Alone
amongst Pacific explorers before Cook, Abel Janszoon Tasman
did not sail "beyond the sunset." Rather, he set new bounds
to the southern continent by sailing from Java and making use
of the Roaring Forties to carry him eastward into the southern
Pacific.

Though the voyage is naturally known by the name of its
commander, the credit for its inception goes to Antonio Van
Diemen, Coen's successor as Governor, and to the navigator
Visscher, who sailed with Tasman, and whose memorandum on
Pacific exploration inspired the Company to take its first (and
last) step towards opening up a route to Chile. Up to this time
the Company had been too busy establishing itself to look
farther afield. Every year it paid enormous dividends, and the
excellence of its charts, maps and topographical sketches in its
Secret Atlas is unrivalled at that date. A lovely map of the
whole of the Pacific by Hessel Gerritsz (Blaeu's predecessor as
the Company's cartographer) is said to exist in the archives of
the Bibliothèque Nationale, and there is a copy at Sydney.

ong the bottom of it, instead of *Terra Australis*, we find a
ging sea with three-masted galleons tossing on the waves.
ips are seen passing and repassing on the Manila route;
tive canoes and the usual mermaids and leviathans enliven
y blank spaces.   Dutch and Spanish discoveries are gaily
arked in yellow and green, and Le Maire's route is boldly
own.   Dr. Wieder, the leading authority on Dutch maps,
tes it provisionally at 1622, and certainly Tasman used it,
cause when he discovered the Fiji and Tonga groups he
agined he had found what Schouten called the Islas de
lomon, so called on this map.

Visscher submitted a number of possibilities for the con-
leration of the Company.   One was to sail south from Java to
. 54°, much farther south than the extremity of the west
ast of New Holland, the old name for Western Australia,
hich was comparatively well known by this date.   If course
as then set east one would be bound to strike the coast of *Terra
ustralis* at some point; it might be that New Holland was
rt of the continent; more likely, the long-sought-for land
y farther east.   Alternatively, if a base was established on the
ast of Chile, one could sail either east or west along the
ttom of the world.

The first of these plans formed the basis of the instructions
ued to Tasman in 1642.   Reduced to its simplest, the idea
as to find out how far south the known coast of Australia
tended.   Was it possible to sail east round the cape dis-
vered by Peter de Nuyts (near modern Perth) and so to
ile?

So Tasman tacked across the Indian Ocean till he found
mself within the limits of the Horse Latitudes.   Here the
esterlies carried him east until (to quote the first English
count of the matter) "the 24th of November 1642, in South
atitude 42d. 25m. and their middle longitude of 163d. 50m.
6° out according to our reckoning) they saw Land E. by N.
stant from them 10 miles, which they named Anthony Van
iemen's Land."   Anchoring in a bay near Hobart, "they
eard as they thought the noise of Men, but saw none, and the

play which they heard was much like that of the Jews-Trum
or little Gom (gong)."

They did not stay long on the shores of what we call Ta
mania because they were sure it was inhabited by giants an
tigers. So, "on December 5 they went away East with purpo
to run away East to the Longitude of 195d. to find the islands
Solomon." What they did find on December 18 was Ne
Zealand. Tasman first named the country Staten Land, for
imagined it was the western edge of *Terra Australis*, of whi
Schouten's Staten Land was the eastern part. When it w
known that the eastern Staten Land had been reduced to t
status of an island, the name Nova Zeelandia was substitute
As such it appears on some of the charts of this voyage, and al
on the huge pavement map in the new Stadthaus at Amsterda
The outlines of that magnificent record of Dutch enterprise we
speedily erased by the footsteps of the thousands who visit
this new glory of the Netherlands; but some idea of it has be
preserved for us by a French visitor, Thevenot, who sketched
in his *Relation des Divers Voyages Curieux* in 1664. He
Zeelandia Nova is shown as part of an undefined *Terre Austra*
"découverte l'an 1644." Actually the year was 1642, an
Tasman sailed right across the area marked *Terre Australe*.

Misliking his entertainment at the hands of the Maoris
Massacre Bay (near Nelson), he tried to continue east, but fin
ing wind and sea against him he went away in a norther
direction. If he had not done so he would have discovered th
what he supposed to be an inlet was really a strait, Cook Stra
and that New Zealand was not part of a continent but a la
eminently suitable for colonisation.

Thus another opportunity was lost and the Southland r
mained a very substantial legend. At all events he proved th
New Holland was not part of it, however vast it might b
because, by sailing north, he rejoined Schouten's route, di
covering the Fiji and Tonga islands on the way. Because
followed the route of his predecessor, he also missed the Sol
mons, now rapidly fading into the mists of fable.

Tasman returned to Java via the north of New Guinea

une 1643 after a ten months' voyage which contributed more
o the knowledge of the world than any save those of Columbus
nd Magellan. He was a fortunate, but not a great, explorer.
The inspiration of the voyage was not his but Visscher's, and
oth on this voyage and the next, when he was sent to see if
New Guinea was joined to New Holland, he made grievous
mistakes. He failed to find Cook Strait and he failed to find
Torres Strait. It looks as if he did not have the patience or the
curiosity of the true explorer. Because he failed to follow every
old in the coast to make sure an inlet is not a strait, he missed
discoveries of the first importance which would otherwise have
been his.

The Company was not impressed by his achievement. In
their view, exploration was legitimate only in so far as it brought
tangible rewards. Tasman, they complained, "has been to some
extent remiss in investigating the situation, conformation and
nature of the lands and peoples discovered, and left the main
part of this task to be executed by some more inquisitive successor." New Holland, boldly identified by some as *Beach
Provincia Aurifera*, was nothing more than the haunt of "wild,
cruel black savages." Earlier reports were now confirmed,
since Tasman "found nothing that could be turned to profit,
but has only come across naked, beach-roving wretches, destitute
even of rice, miserably poor, and in many places of a very bad
disposition."

So Australia remained a scratch on the map—*terre de coste
dangereuse*—a fairly accurate scratch as far as the north and west
coasts were concerned, but with nothing at all to the east or the
south, save the little angle of land seen in 1642 (not until 1798
was it found that Tasmania was really an island). Far to the east
of it ran a thread of coastline called New Zealand, generally
regarded as the western edge of *Terra Australis*, still *Incognita*.
The monopoly of the Company was sufficiently rich and secure
to permit them concentrating on the Indies and the lands to the
north. "I have heard it said among the Dutch," wrote our
ambassador in the reign of Charles II, "that their East-India
Company have long since forbidden any further attempts of

discovering that continent, having already more trade in thos
parts than they can turn to account, and fearing some mor
populous nation of Europe might make great establishments c
trade in some of these unknown regions, which might ruin c
impair what they have already in the Indies.''

There was a time when the Dutch West India Company bi
fair to rival the prosperity of their East India Company. Thei
ships once captured the Plate Fleet, and their settlements in th
West Indies and South America proved highly successful. To
wards the end of the seventeenth century, many years afte
Tasman's voyage had been to all intents and purposes forgotten
"a Gentleman of great Parts and Penetration" named Rogge
veen (or Roggewein) submitted to this Company a scheme fo:
discovering "southern lands." The moment was not propitious
for the country was impoverished by prolonged wars agains
France and Britain. On his deathbed Roggeveen made his soi
Jacob promise that he would press the project when time:
improved. Jacob did so, after a long interval during which he
rose to high office in the East and retired with a fortune at the
age of 62. In 1721, seventy-eight years after Tasman had made
the last Dutch voyage in the Pacific, he approached the West
India Company again. This time the Company agreed and
three ships were commissioned—*Eagle*, *Tienhoven* and *African*
Galley. At his time of life Jacob might have retired to smoke
his pipe in peace and send others to brave the hardships of such
a voyage, but he preferred to honour the promise made to his
father, and he himself embarked as commander.

They reached the Straits without incident, save for an example of savage discipline at sea which is remarkable even in
that age and that profession. A swabber, suffering from extreme
pangs of thirst, broached a cask of brandy and threatened the
cook with a knife when reprimanded. For this he was keel-
hauled—i.e. thrown over one side of the ship and hoisted up
half-drowned on the other—flogged with 300 lashes, salt rubbed
into the cuts, then nailed to the foremast with a knife through
the palm of his hand to starve to death. If he had not died
before land was sighted they proposed to maroon him.

Passing through the Straits they were driven as far south as
?° 50', where the ships were in hourly danger of being im-
isoned by ice floes. But they managed to make Juan Fer-
ndez, about which Roggeveen waxed enthusiastic. Like
any another explorer at that date, he thought it an ideal South
a base, a springboard for attacks on the decadent provinces of
anish South America. This he considered "the best laid
heme for promoting southern discoveries that ever yet entered
e head of man." He decided to follow it up on his return.
eanwhile he pressed on in search of *Terra Australis*, which
 estimated to lie between latitudes 50° and 56° S. He had
ad reports of an island said to have been seen by an English
ccaneer, Captain Davis, in 28° S. However, "much to the
tonishment of the admiral, we could not find Davis Land."
pon which they came to the correct conclusion that the English
ccaneers "must have been rovers from truth as well as rovers
er the goods of the Spaniards."

Their first landfall, and their only genuine discovery, on
ster Day, 1722, was the most mysterious of all Pacific Islands,
ich they named Easter Island: the island of a hundred
eories and the home of those sinister, sphinx-like giant faces,
o of which used to stand at the portals of the British Museum
ring out into London grime, far from the wild waters of their
tive coast. The Dutchmen were more interested in the heavy
-rings worn by the islanders, which stretched their lobes
wn to their shoulders, and their peace offerings of 500 live
vls and as many women as they liked to take on board.
termined to find giants wherever they went, one writer
ists that he saw men twelve feet tall. He goes on to describe,
th tantalising vagueness, the worship of the monstrous stone
ls which dotted the island. When a cannon was fired the
tives jumped about, pointing first to the visitors and then to
 statues, appealing for vengeance with howls of *Dago! Dago!*
ne of the early visitors throw much light on these monu-
nts, the origin of which is lost in the prehistoric past. Whence
ne the labour and the skill and the materials to carve and
ct those 70-foot monsters? Why did work upon them stop

so suddenly, the crude tools thrown aside as if the news of catastrophe suddenly interrupted the sculptors? If we acce the theory of Macmillan Brown, there was indeed once a gre southern continent, or at any rate an immense archipelag stretching from the Marianas to Easter Island, which has sin subsided. According to him, Davis Land really existed but w submerged before Roggeveen arrived in those parts. His co clusions have been the subject of much criticism, and East Island remains the island of mystery.

Leaving Easter Island, Roggeveen crossed Schouten's tra and sailed across the ocean by a parallel but slightly mo northerly course. Later he admitted his mistake: "I am firm persuaded that if we had stood to the S.W. we could not ha failed to discover some land." So Schouten's track alo 15°-20° S. remained the most southerly yet.

Their course soon brought them among the islets of Tuamo Archipelago. The *African Galley* ran upon a coral reef su rounding one of these earthly paradises, whereupon Roggeve named it Pernicious Island. Emerging from what he calls t Labyrinth, they found Recreation Island, one of the islands ju north of Tahiti. At this point, as happened so often in the voyages, all thoughts of further discovery were suddenly aba doned. All we know is that Roggeveen read his commission his officers, by which it was apparent that, if no land was se in the position they were in, they should make for Java. Ma showed their surprise that having come so far to discover *Ter Australis* they should not make more effort to do so. But, li Schouten, Roggeveen seems to have lost his nerve. If more m continued to die of scurvy at the rate they were doing, he fear that the ships would become unmanageable; since they mu have provisioned with fresh fruit and vegetables at the islan they had so recently passed, this seems a poor excuse. Mo likely, as one disgruntled version has it, "the true cause of sudden a change and so precipitate a return, was the anxie which the greatest part of the officers had to go to the East Indi They were afraid to lose their monsoon by further delay."

So they returned via the north of New Guinea, as their pr

ecessors had done in the previous century, making a few fresh
iscoveries among the lovely Samoan Islands on the way.   On
rrival at Batavia they met, as they ought to have expected, the
ame fate as Schouten and Le Maire had suffered a century
efore.   Their ships were seized and they themselves arrested
s interlopers by the officials of the rival Company.   In this way
ne voyage of the last of the Dutch explorers ends with old
oggeveen being sent home under arrest.   The merchants
emained secure in their rich dominion until the coming of the
apanese in our own day.

THE BUCCANEERS IN THE SOUTH SEAS

BETWEEN Sir Richard Hawkins' *Dainty* in 1594 and Sir John Narborough's *Sweepstakes* in 1670 no English ship sailed into the Pacific. A few schemes, such as Sir William Courteen's petition for a grant of "all lands in ye south parts of ye world called *Terra Australis, incognita*" in 1624, never got farther than the paper stage. Until the appearance of the buccaneers in those seas towards the end of the seventeenth century, the story of English enterprise in that part of the world is a blank.

Narborough's voyage itself is an isolated episode, on account of the hostility it aroused on the part of Spain. Alone of Stuart enterprises in the Pacific it had official backing. None the less it is hard to say who was responsible for it;—possibly Pepys because we know that he had a great admiration for Narborough among the naval commanders of the day. Two naval ships were used, and according to the printed instructions Narborough's aim was to explore the coast of Chile with a view to laying the foundations of a trade there, though every precaution was to be taken to avoid meddling with Spanish settlements. On the other hand, Greenville Collins, the talented hydrographer who sailed with him, gives an additional objective which savours of Tudor times: a search for the western exit of the North-West Passage. Narborough's failure to make any attempt to do so is excused on the grounds of "the cowardice of our consort," the *Bachelor* pink, which deserted off Patagonia. But his own conduct once he reached the Pacific was so unenterprising we may well doubt if he ever intended to obey his original instructions

The *Sweepstakes* was well manned, well armed, and well victualled ("$4\frac{1}{2}$ tons of brandy in lieu of beer"), carrying a cargo of knives, cloth and tobacco, when she sailed from England in 1669. Her commander was a man of scientific bent, typical of his age. Narborough measured the Patagonians to see if they vere giants, and found them "not above the common bigness of men"; he salted penguins and tried to preserve 100,000 eggs or provisions; he tested the soil, found the climate healthy, and carefully described anything new in the way of fishes or animals. Englishmen were introduced to the skunk, for example, under the name of "huffer," "because when he sets right upon you, he will stand vapouring and patting with his fore feet upon the ground, yet hath no manner of defence for himself, but with his breech; for upon your approach, he turns about and makes the most abominable stink in the world." The most valuable result of the expedition was a new chart of the Straits of Magellan—so accurate that it enabled the mutineers of the *Wager* on Anson's voyage, seventy years later, to make their way back in a longboat.

Narborough soon found himself on the tracks of his predecessors. At Port Desire he found a leaden plate and a box, containing an indecipherable paper, left by Le Maire half a century before. At St. Julian he found bones which he supposed were those of Drake's mutineers. Through the Straits he used the only chart made by an English sailor, John Davis of Dartmouth. But once in the Pacific his behaviour was far different to that of the Elizabethans. At Valdivia he was politely asked whither he was bound? To China, he replied. But the way he began to press for information about the coast led his Spanish hosts to suspect the honesty of his intentions. A shore party, consisting of four men, was detained and no explanation given when their release was requested under flag of truce. Without making any further effort to rescue his men or fulfil the aims of the expedition, Narborough turned back for home. He had only been on the coast a week. Perhaps yet another Elizabethan precedent was fresh in his mind: the treachery of the Spaniards towards Sir John Hawkins at S. Juan Ulloa.

The real revival of interest in the South Seas was due to the buccaneers, for no official expedition was again sent to these parts before that of Anson seventy years later. These freebooters, *flibustiers, zee roovers* (rascals of every nationality except Spain, the traditional enemy) were descended from the pirates

of the Caribbean area. Their behaviour may not have bee
quite so eccentric as that of the romantic villains who chewe
glass, stuck lighted matches in their hair, roasted prisoners ove
a slow fire, or extorted information by sticking needles dow
their finger nails. Nevertheless, they were reared in the sam
nursery; many of them were tried for piracy, and most of thei
ships were seized from countries with which we were nominall
at peace. Their roystering habits, their deep potations of run
punch punctuated by the firing of guns, the way they depose
their captains at will and acted mutinously whenever they fe
so inclined, mark them as belonging to the true pirate breed
If they have any common distinguishing mark it is the anti
Spanish feeling which animated all their activities. The tru
pirate plundered friend and foe alike; the buccaneer, thoug
indeed a sea robber, usually at least confined his depredation
to Spanish waters.

Buccaneers are not, however, to be confused with genuin
privateers, who carried a government commission in thei
cabins, and who were responsible to the owners for the conduc
of their ships. To a privateer like Woodes Rogers the buc
caneers were "a hellish company," though that did not dete
him from employing their skill as navigators. Notwithstanding
this eminently respectable attitude, it often happened that
ship which sailed from England a commissioned private man
of-war was transformed into a pirate as soon as her commande
reached latitudes in which he felt himself secure from the eye
of his owners or his government. Legally, the distinctio
between pirate and privateer depended on whether a state o
peace or war existed at any given moment, and whether th
voyage had been sanctioned by a government or not; but t
those who sailed the South Seas these were questions of merel
academic importance.

Of course, the buccaneers tried to pose as anything but wha
they really were. One captain who touched at Guam described
his band of cut-throats as "employ'd by some Gentlemen o
France upon discovery of those unknown Parts of the World."
A forged or stolen commission often eased the situation. But

abricated excuses could be dispensed with when one found
oneself in a strong position.   When the Governor of Panama
asked to see Captain Sawkins' commission, the latter replied:
"We would come and visit him and bring our commissions on
the muzzles of our guns, at which time he should read them as
plain as the flames of gunpowder could make them."

The migration of the buccaneers from the Caribbean into
the Pacific begins with the 330 men who crossed the isthmus
under Captains Sawkins, Sharp and Coxon in 1680.   "Being
all Souldiers of Fortune," writes Captain Sharp, "'Twas Gold
was the bait that tempted a Pack of merry Boys of us."   For
the next six years scores of them sailed up and down the coast,
using Juan Fernandez and the Galapagos Islands off Peru as
bases, plundering by sea and by land whenever opportunity
offered.   Constantly they broke up into fresh units, regrouping
themselves under more enterprising leaders, drifting hither and
thither as the scent of plunder attracted them.   Sea tramps by
nature, they were never satisfied with one captain or one place
for long.   Some few, like flotsam, drifted across the ocean for
no other reason than a desire to see what lay on the other side.
One at least went round the world three times.

There was a moment when this international force, nearly
a thousand strong, ruled the South Seas, but the usual inter-
necine jealousies made it a brief one.   For sheer impudence
their letter to the Governor of Panama deserves attention.

If you refuse this last demand and thinke that the im-
prisonement of three or foure Englishmen is more advantageous to you than the lives of soe many of your Countrymen
as are already and what else shall fall into our hands, then
you may keep them and we will send you the heads of these
for a beginning; and then doe our Countrymen the least
hurt in their lives or bodyes and by the helpe of God wee will
colour your Land Rivers and sea with Spanish blood of men
women and children the whole time that wee remaine in
these seas, turning our former Mercy into cruelty, shewing
mercy nor giving quarter to any.

wee will bring our ships near your walls that you may
have the pleasure of seeing them (the Spanish prisoners
hanged at our yard armes.

wee will make you know that wee are the Commanders
of the whole South Seas, so consider what to choose for wee
waite your sentence of life or death with impatience, if death
you shall certainly have the heads by Monday morning.

From the Comanders of the whole South Seas
Feb. 22. 1685.

As far as exploration is concerned their record is not impressive. They sailed without charts, by guess and by God (or
perhaps one should say, with the luck of the Devil). Experience
turned them perforce into skilful navigators, and, since their
aim was plunder, they preferred the more frequented trade
routes, only disappearing into hidden havens when danger
threatened. Sailing in haphazard manner, chance must have
compelled them to make fresh discoveries if any such remained
off these coasts. But the only thing left for them to do was to
rename certain earlier discoveries. Thus the group south of
the Marianas acquired the modern name of Carolines, and the
Falklands became so named from an extension of the name
Falkland Sound, which the privateer Strong applied to one of
the bays in 1698.

Their taste was for islands, but those they claimed to have
discovered invariably proved illusory. We have seen how Davis
Land (thought by some of his shipmates to be part of *Terra
Australis*) was the will-o'-the-wisp which led Roggeveen to discover Easter Island. Captain Ambrosia Cowley left an attractive
description of what came to be called Pepys Island in the
Atlantic, and half a dozen later explorers wasted time trying to
track down this phantom. Better still, and quite in keeping
with his Christian name, was the vision he saw near the Galapagos, "which my Fancy led me to call *Cowley's Enchanted
Island*; for we having had a sight of it upon several Points of
the Compass, it appear'd always in as many different Forms;

ometimes like a ruined Fortification; upon another Point,
ike a great City." . . .

"*Sometimes we see a cloud that's dragonish.*"

The reason why such an irresponsible crowd of drunken
profligates had such a tremendous influence on the history of
exploration is because there happened to be on board a natural
genius, one of the most attractive personalities to be met with
n any book of travel. William Dampier is at first obscured by
his louder shipmates, for he sailed in a very subordinate capacity
with the first invaders of the South Seas. Gradually the figure
emerges, until, with the publication of his journals in 1697, he
stands out as a person of remarkable charm and talent. As an
observer, his accuracy would do credit to any field-working
scientist; as a writer, he stands in the very first class.

If ever a man was born a rolling stone it was Dampier. Bred
to a trade in a Somerset village, he turned his back on the
prospect of so modest a livelihood to go to sea. A voyage to the
Newfoundland Banks proved to his own satisfaction that he
did not like cold latitudes, so he went on a voyage to India.
After service in the Dutch wars he accepted the post of manager
of a West India plantation, but he threw it up to join the
hard-drinking band of log-cutters in the Bay of Campeachy
(Honduras). In this nursery of buccaneers he easily found the
opportunity to cross the isthmus to join the rovers in the South
Seas. Thence he went round the world, not once but three
times. It took him eight years (1683-1691) to make his first
voyage. Having left the original band led by Sharp, he returned to Virginia where he shipped with Captains Davis,
Cowley and Cook to rejoin their comrades in the Pacific. He
tactfully omits to mention that their ship, the *Batchelour's
Delight*, "a lovely ship" of 40 guns, was a piratical seizure.
It was intended to sail through the Straits of Magellan, but
Dampier dissuaded his captain on the grounds that it was too
hazardous a piece of navigation for such an ill-disciplined
crew. So they rounded the Horn and joined up with a certain
Captain Swan, whose ship was named, by a pretty conceit, the
Cygnet. After cruising about for some weeks Dampier, in

casual buccaneering fashion, decided to shift to the *Cygnet*— "not from any dislike to my old Captain, but to get some knowledge of the Northern Parts," for, he admits, "I came into these seas this second time more to endulge my cureosity than to gett wealth."

The Pacific he thought well named, as long as the name was applied to that part of the ocean lying between 4° and 30° S. Compared with other seas, it was innocent of hurricanes and gales, with only the steady Trade winds blowing. As to entrances to it, he favoured the Horn route, though he admits the possibility of a North-West Passage. New Holland, he thought, might prove to be part of *Terra Australis*, and possibly Davis Land was another part of it. The way to settle the question was obviously to go and look for it, and he blames those trading with the Philippines for the continued existence of the mystery. If one was not a Spaniard and one wished to do business in the Philippines he advised a westerly route via the Horn, making use of the S.E. Trades to cross the Pacific. For the return instead of using the northern Westerlies, as the Spaniards did, the Englishman should sail south into the Horse Latitudes, and so east to Patagonia. "To speak my Thoughts freely, I believe 'tis owing to the neglect of this easie way that all that vast tract of *Terra Australis* which bounds the South Sea is yet undiscovered." Cook, on his second voyage, was to prove the truth of this observation, and Dampier was thus the first to suggest the famous route by which the wool clippers sailed from Australia in the nineteenth century.

However, buccaneers had to make a living, and to do that they had to follow frequented trade routes. So when Captain Swan found prizes becoming scarce in the coastwise trade off Mexico, he decided to stretch across to the farther side of the ocean to seek his fortune there. Of course Dampier applauded the decision; indeed, as navigator, he may have been partly responsible for it; but Swan had great difficulty in persuading his 150 men to follow him, such was the fear this great gulf aroused even in such hardy hearts as theirs. "Such was their Ignorance," smiles Dampier, "they thought he would carry

hem out of the world." The crossing in the belt of the N.E.
Trades proved easier than had been anticipated. "We made
great Runs every Day," the best being 216 miles. He gives
interesting statistics about the voyage from Mexico to Guam.
The time taken was 52 days; and from the sum of their west-
ings, 7323 miles, or 125° 11', he was able to correct current
misconceptions about the breadth of the ocean.

They reached Guam just in time, for they had only three
days' provisions left. "As I was afterwards informed, the Men
had contrived, first to kill Capt. *Swan* and eat him when the
Victuals was gone, and after him all of us who were accessory
in promoting the undertaking of this Voyage. This made Capt.
Swan say to me after our arrival at Guam, '*Ah! Dampier, you
would have made them but a poor Meal*'; for I was as lean as
the Captain was lusty and fleshy."

Continuing west to the Philippines, they found themselves
in a land flowing with milk and honey, the disciplinary effect
of which was worse than that of the privations of the crossing.
Idleness bred drunkenness, drunkenness led to dallying with
native women, and that begot trouble with jealous husbands,
as well as quarrels amongst themselves. Dampier's dislike of
the "mad crew," and his taste for wandering, forced him to
consort with those mutineers who planned to seize a ship
and sail away. Without compunction, the majority, including
Captain Swan, who was now behaving like a swaggering bully,
were left to the mercies of the jealous husbands, by whom they
were later killed. Quite casually the deserters decided to
"touch at New Holland, a part of *Terra Australis*, to see what
that Country would afford us."

It afforded them very little. Both on this occasion and on
his subsequent voyage in the *Roebuck*, Dampier only visited
the inhospitable north-western shores, and, like his Dutch
predecessors, he was not favourably impressed by the "blinking
savages" who inhabited what he supposed to be the great Southland. A passage in which he describes them is worth quoting,
not only because it is an admirable example of his style, but
because it gave Swift a hint for the *Yahoos*.

The Inhabitants of this Country are the miserablest Peopl
in the World. The Hodmadods of Monomatapa, though
nasty People, yet for Wealth are Gentlemen to these; wh
have no houses or skin Garments, Sheep, Poultry, and Fruit
of the Earth, Ostrich Eggs, etc. as the Hodmadods have: An
setting aside their Humane Shape, they differ but little from
Brutes. They are tall, strait-bodied, and thin, with smal
long Limbs. They have great Heads, round Foreheads, an
great Brows. Their Eye-lids are always half closed, to kee
the Flies out of their Eyes; they being so troublesome here
that no Fanning will keep them from coming to ones Face
and without the assistance of both Hands to keep them off
they will creep into ones Nostrils, and Mouth too, if the Lip
are not shut very close; so that from their Infancy being
thus annoyed with these Insects, they do never open their
Eyes as other People: And therefore they cannot see far
unless they hold up their Heads, as if they were looking a
somewhat over them.

They have great Bottle Noses, pretty full Lips, and wide
Mouths. The two Fore-teeth of their Upper Jaw are wanting
in all of them, Men and Women, Old and Young; whether
they draw them out, I know not: Neither have they any
Beards. They are long visaged, and of a very unpleasing
Aspect, having no one graceful Feature in their Faces.

Such were the impressions of the first Englishman to visit
Australia: it is not surprising that his readers were more en-
tranced by the glamour of the unknown *Terra Australis* than
by the realities of what we call Australia. His subsequent
adventures, including dangers with which those he had previously encountered were "but a play-game in comparison," do
not concern us. In devious fashion he worked a passage home
with nothing to show for all his adventures but his precious
journal, which he had somehow preserved, even though, on
occasion, it had to be carried in a hollow bamboo; and his
Painted Prince, a tattooed Malay called Jeoly, whom he "carried
about for a shew, till he died of the Small-Pox at Oxford."

For the next few years he lived in obscurity, assiduously preparing his manuscript for publication. When it appeared in 1697 its success was immediate. In consequence of dedicating it to the President of the Royal Society, the ex-buccaneer was lionised by all those interested in the arts and sciences. Pepys asked him to a dinner party at which Evelyn was present. The latter was very favourably impressed by the modest behaviour of this representative of such legendary monsters; unfortunately Pepys was too blind to record his reactions.

As a result of an introduction to the First Lord of the Admiralty, Dampier found himself in the odd position of being offered the command of one of His Majesty's ships of war to go and discover the southern continent. First he was given the *Jolly Prize*, but when this was found to be totally unsuitable for a voyage of this type he was offered the *Roebuck*, a little ship recently fitted out as a fireship. She was in such terrible condition that she "founder'd thro' perfect Age" on the way back. Evidently the authorities were not prepared to spend much trouble or money on the enterprise. Poor Dampier was put in command of a worm-eaten hulk manned by a discontented crew, whose officers were at no pains to hide their disgust at having to serve under an ex-buccaneer. A few weeks out he had to confine his first lieutenant to his cabin, and then left him unceremoniously ashore at Brazil, because he went about calling his captain "old Rogue, old Dog, old Cheat." For this Dampier was court-martialled on his return in 1702 by a court consisting of four admirals and thirty-three captains. A man of his record stood little chance in a court so constituted. But it must be a unique occurrence in the history of courts-martial that the President, Sir George Rooke, condemned a man who had just returned from naming a new island in his honour, to forfeit all his pay. In addition, Dampier was found "not a fitt person to be Employ'd as commander of any of Her Majesty's ships."

On this voyage, which lasted from 1699 to 1702, Dampier had originally intended to follow his own advice and take the Horn route. Delays on the part of the Navy Board made this

impossible, so he reached New Holland by way of the Cape o
Good Hope. Thence, using "Mr. Tasman's draught," h
coasted round the north of New Guinea until he came to th
limit of charted waters. At this point he was off what we cal
New Ireland. Finding that the coast trended away to th
south, he followed it until the rotten state of his ship and th
grumblings of his crew forced him to give up the search for th
continent. The coast he was following was a fresh discovery
New Britain, he called it, leaving many English names along it
—Cape Orford, Port Montagu, Cape Anne, Cape Gloster. Bu
what he marks in his map as St. George's Bay is really a strai
in which lies the harbour of Rabaul. A century later Cartere
discovered this strait, and since Dampier had named the souther
island New Britain, he named the northern one New Ireland.

For an island New Britain proved to be. Dampier foun
that the coast turned sharply west and that he was able to sai
between his discovery and New Guinea. New Britain, and th
passage between it and New Guinea which bears his nam
form the sum of Dampier's achievements, as far as discover
is concerned. But for the accident of being provided with
rotten ship and a worse crew, his name might have bee
numbered among the greatest explorers of all time. He knev
what to look for, and where to look for it, but his inability t
surmount the deficiencies put in his way by the authoritie
prevented him from finding it. However, the proceeds from
his *Voyage to New Holland* compensated him for the loss o
the pittance he should have been paid.

Fortunately for him, private shipowners of those days wer
not over scrupulous about the credentials of a commander of
privateer to operate in the South Seas. The War of the Spanisl
Succession had now begun, so that a year after his return h
had no difficulty in finding a ship, the *St. George* of 26 guns
with which sailed the *Cinque Ports* (Capt. Stradling) of 16 guns
But the *St. George* was as rotten as the *Roebuck*, and for th
second time Dampier proved himself an incompetent com
mander, possibly a dishonest one as well.

Of this new venture, which lasted from 1703 till 1707, w

only have accounts by professed enemies and his own intemper-
ate vindication. Both Funnell, who describes himself as a mate
whereas he was only a steward, and midshipman Welbe, charge
Dampier with failings which do not square with what we know
of him from other sources. The face we see in the fine portrait here reproduced (p. 75) is not the face of a bully. But
Welbe declares that he was habitually drunk and abusive, calling
his men "rogues, rascals, and sons of bitches." For his part,
Dampier frequently expresses his abhorrence of drunkenness,
and calls his present crew "a parcel of fellows who were per-
petually drunk." Perhaps the truth is that the effects of his
buccaneering education became apparent once he got to sea,
or else that he was incapable of concealing his intellectual
superiority over the sort of seamen with whom he sailed.
Evelyn was attracted by his modesty; but Swift describes the
Captain Pocock (in reality Dampier) whom Lemuel Gulliver
meets on his last voyage as "an honest man, and a good sailor,
but a little too positive in his own opinions, which was the
cause of his destruction as it had been of several others."
Perhaps that was the secret of his ill-success.

Whatever it was, the catastrophic cruise of the *St. George*
proved once more that he did not possess what are mysteriously
termed "officer-like qualities." To answer the charge of
cowardice it is sufficient to recall the state of his ship, through
the worm-eaten timbers of which he could push his finger, and
the way in which he was deserted by his consort and by the
majority of his crew (including Funnell). The incident in
which he is specially accused was a brush with some French
corsairs off Juan Fernandez. Dampier's explanation of what
happened is that the opening broadside "Dismay'd my Men
so much, they actually run down off the Deck, and made
nothing of it afterwards, so that when I could have boarded her
and carried her, the Mate, Cleppington by Name (Clipperton,
who later deserted with twenty-two men), cry'd *The Men are
all gone*; and Bellhash the Master, whose Office it was to be
always upon Deck, was gone also; tho' this Gentleman is now
a Valiant Talker, to my Detriment."

G

Welbe also declares that, had it not been for Dampier's incompetence, they could have captured the Manila galleon farther north. But with the *St. George* in such a state that she had to be abandoned shortly afterwards her captain was well advised not to press an action.

By this date the *Cinque Ports* had deserted, having narrowly escaped capture at the hands of some St. Malo corsairs engaged by the Spaniards "to search for our English enemies which infest the South Seas." At Juan Fernandez her sailing master, the famous Alexander Selkirk, was left behind at his own request, not, as is usually stated, marooned. Stradling himself suffered shipwreck farther north. He was carried back to France, where he lay manacled in a pit in Dinan prison for five years, before he succeeded in fooling his gaolers with stories about buried treasure on the coast of Peru and escaping by a rope of sheets.

After abandoning the *St. George*, Dampier wished to cross the Pacific in a brigantine prize, following the same route as he had taken with Swan ten years before. Welbe says he announced the proposal by piping all hands on deck and asking "Who would stay with him to get Money? For his part he came with that Design, and did not intend to go out of the Seas 'till he got some." Someone asked if he proposed to hand over the plunder to the owners, or whether he intended to share the proceeds among the crew? Dampier appears to have implied the latter, claiming that he was protected by a commission from the Queen. The truth is that he had fallen a prey to the very temptation against which he had warned the naval authorities before setting out on his last voyage: "the Temptation our Seamen have had of late to break loose and turn pirate when they came into the nither parts of the World."

Twenty-seven men agreed to sail with him, but fifty-six preferred to leave, declaring that he would never get across with that crew—and indeed, says Dampier, "it is a Miracle in Nature how I did." Nevertheless, he rounded the world a second time, even though his prize was confiscated and he himself imprisoned for a time by the Dutch at Batavia.

His third and last circumnavigation (1708-1711) was more successful, chiefly because he sailed in the subordinate capacity of "pilot for the South Seas." Furthermore, this was the only voyage in which he returned to England in the same ship as he set out.

The ships chartered for this expedition were two well-found and well-armed privateers, named the *Duke* (320 tons) and the *Duchess* (260 tons), commanded by Captain Woodes Rogers. As they approached Juan Fernandez the crew noticed the smoke of a fire, evidently a distress signal. It had been lit by Selkirk, whom they met curiously attired in goatskins. After nearly five years' isolation, says Rogers, "for want of use he spoke his words by halves." An ex-buccaneer named Cook, who was on board as second in command, says that when Selkirk heard that "a certain officer" was with them he wanted to return to his island, and that it was with difficulty he was persuaded to cease being monarch of all he surveyed. The officer in question has been identified with Dampier; but it was Stradling, not Dampier, with whom Selkirk originally quarrelled, and it was Dampier who gave him a testimonial on the strength of which he was signed on as mate on board the *Duchess*.

As with all privateering ventures, their cruise up the coast and across to Guam was carried out in accordance with Elizabethan precedents. The same towns were burned, the same silver looted, and almost the same galleon captured—the smaller Manila ship, the larger one beating off their attack. And just as Drake's habit of dining off silver plate to the music of violins so much endears him to us, so does Rogers' celebration of St. Valentine's Day in mid-ocean. Having drawn up a list "of the fair ladies of Bristol, I sent for my officers into my cabin, where everyone drew and drank the lady's health in a cup of punch, and to a happy sight of 'em all; this I did to put 'em in mind of home." (Captain Cowley did the same thing off the Horn, with disastrous results. While he and his buccaneers were "chusing of Valentines, and discoursing of the Intrigues of Women, there arose a prodigious Storm, driving us into the lat. of 60 deg. and 30 min. South, which is farther than any ship hath sailed before South; so that we concluded the discoursing of Women at Sea was very unlucky, and occasioned the Storm.")

Dampier, who had sailed with Cowley, found things better managed in Rogers' ship. Batavia, too, instead of being a place where they threw you into prison as a pirate, proved "a glorious place for Punch." And alone of his voyages, the expedition was a financial success. It cost £14,000 to fit out, but Rogers returned with "a hundred tons of gold," besides two silver candlesticks still in Bristol Cathedral. It was a happy conclusion to a rambling life. Dampier was now a man of sixty with three outstanding books and three circumnavigations to his credit. Clearly, it was time to retire. After an unsuccessful lawsuit to obtain a larger share of the prize money, he died four years later.

Sailors and readers have united in praise of him. The style of his prose has charmed generations of readers from the time of Swift to that of Masefield. Of course, those who look for respectable virtues like leadership and honesty may be disappointed, for what can only be called very bad company in youth can hardly be expected to produce an efficient executive officer. But everything can be forgiven the man who wrote the best book about the South Sea, to the inspiration of which may be traced the final search for the great Southland.

If Dampier put the Pacific on the map again, and Selkirk produced a whole gallery of Crusoes, Shelvocke, the last of the Pacific privateers, was the man who provided the hint for the story of the Ancient Mariner. His voyage was obviously inspired by the resounding success of Woodes Rogers ten years before him. In 1718, taking advantage of a brief state of war with Spain, certain persons of distinction and merchants of the city of London decided to plunder the Pacific Coast, and thus "put their seafaring friends into a promising imployment." Their claim to be animated by a high-minded desire to be better acquainted with the navigation of that part of the world may be discounted in view of the character of the said seafaring friends, for the chief interest of the voyage is the way it illustrates how narrow were the bounds which divided privateering from piracy.

Originally Shelvocke, who had seen service in the Navy, was put in command of the ships *Success* and *Speedwell*, but his behaviour proved so unsatisfactory before the start that Dampier's mate, Clipperton, was given the supreme command. Being relegated to the smaller ship, the *Speedwell*, Shelvocke took the first opportunity to part company with his superior officer; of course he blames the weather and the dishonesty of Clipperton's intentions for what occurred. According to him, everything went wrong from the start; unfortunately for his story, William Betagh, captain of marines on board the *Speedwell*, survived to write a damaging commentary on his story when it was published in 1726.

The entry into the Pacific was made round the Horn. His description of the "most uncomfortable landskip" of Staten Island, with its snowy cliffs wreathed in mists, the piercing winds bringing snow and sleet, the icebergs encountered, are concentrated in the crucible of the poet's imagination into

> And now there came both mist and snow,
> And it grew wondrous cold;
> And ice, mast-high, came floating by,
> As green as emerald.
>
> And through the drifts the snowy clifts
> Did send a dismal sheen:
> Nor shapes of men nor beasts we ken—
> The ice was all between.

It was here that Simon Hatley, late mate of the *Duchess*, shot the albatross. "We had not had sight of one fish of any kind, since we were come to the Southward of the streights of Le Maire, nor one sea-bird, except a disconsolate black *Albatross*, who accompanied us for several days, hovering about us as if he had lost himself, till Hatley (my second captain), observing, in one of his melancholy fits, that this bird was always hovering near us, imagined, from his colour, that it might be some ill omen. That which, I suppose, induced him the more to

encourage his superstition, was the continual series of contrary
tempestuous winds, which had oppressed us ever since we had
got into this sea.   But be that as it would, he, after some fruitless
attempts, at length shot the *Albatross*, not doubting (perhaps)
that we should have a fair wind after it."

By slow degrees they crept northwards to Juan Fernandez,
where Shelvocke professed to think that Clipperton would be
waiting.   Of course he was not there, so they embarked under
French colours on a cruise up and down the coast.   Shelvocke's
favourite custom was to capture a prize and then demand
ransom (in gold or silver) at the point of a gun;   sometimes he
succeeded, but often the Spaniards merely shrugged their
shoulders and watched him burn their wretched ships in peevish
disappointment.   Payta was sacked, as it had been many times
before and was to be again.   Then Shelvocke returned to Juan
Fernandez in order to refit.   However, soon after he got there
the *Speedwell* was cast away on some rocks, according to Betagh
on purpose to defraud the owners.   Finding that "everything
that one sees or hears in this place is perfectly romantick" (an
early example of the use of this word in its modern sense), his
thoughts may well have turned to the delights of a buccaneering
cruise, of doing what Dampier would have liked to have done
when he abandoned the *St. George*.   According to him, his
men decided the question by mutinying, deposing him from his
position, allowing him six instead of the customary sixty shares
in the loot, and declaring they were their own masters.   They
then proceeded to quarrel amongst themselves, and each side
in turn begged Shelvocke to resume command.

A boat of sorts was built and the pirate band set out to seize
the first ship they could find to replace their own crazy craft.
Having done so, they looted what was left of Payta and cruised
north to the Mexican coast.   Here, by the merest chance, they
fell in with the *Success*, but met with a very cool reception.
It was clear to all those on board Clipperton's vessel that Shelvocke's men had turned pirate.   Says the chief mate of the
Success, "they have quite broke their articles with the owners,
and have shared all among themselves."   At that date pirates

were being regularly executed at home, so the law-abiding
privateers, as Shelvocke complains, "were unwilling to have
anything to say or do with me." Having handed over some
ammunition, Clipperton sheered off next day, and though they
occasionally met during the next few weeks, sometimes passing
so near each other that a biscuit might have been tossed from
one ship to another, they were no longer on speaking terms.
Shelvocke, however, met with more success than he deserved,
as one of the ships he captured was found to be carrying 100,000
dollars in coin on board. He was informed by the Spanish
authorities that peace had been signed, so he promptly put to
sea again with his prize. There was nothing for it but to cross
the Pacific.

The voyage took him twice as long as he expected from a
reading of Dampier's account, and his men suffered so badly
from scurvy that he dared not stop at Guam to refresh them,
in case he should be attacked in his present weak state. In
November 1721 he anchored in the Canton river, only to find
the *Success* already there before him. For a final fling at his
rivals, he relates how Clipperton ran his ship on shore in an
attempt to take a prize, and that to animate himself against
the spirited fire of the enemy he had recourse to brandy to such
an extent "that he in an instant became dead drunk, and
tumbled on the deck, and snored out his time in a beastly
manner, whilst his first lieutenant Davidson undertook the
command of the ship, which he bravely executed till he was
killed." As soon as the engagement was broken off, his men
locked him in his cabin and deserted.

Shelvocke's crew did very much the same, so he sold the
ship and took a passage home in an East Indiaman. But that
was not the end of this sorry venture, for the owners had him
arrested on charges ranging from piracy to fraud. In the
distribution of the prize money at Macao each man received
1887 dollars, Shelvocke reserving for his own share 11,325;
that left at least 10,000 unaccounted for, apart from the trans-
parently fraudulent arrangement he made with the Chinese
over the sale of the ship. Shelvocke obtained bail and fled the

country. To save the family reputation his brother-in-law
made some sort of composition with the owners, but Betagh
concludes his commentary in the confident hope that his late
captain would soon be caught and tried for piracy.

One day in the autumn of 1797 Coleridge, Wordsworth and
Dorothy set out to walk over the Quantocks to Lynton. To
defray their expenses they proposed to write a poem; casting
about for a subject Wordsworth mentioned that he had lately
been reading Shelvocke's narrative in which he was struck by
the episode of Hatley and the albatross. From Professor Living-
stone Lowes' researches we know how extraordinary was
Coleridge's appetite for the old voyagers. As if by magic, the
mass of miscellaneous knowledge he had gathered in his mind
was fired by the hint Wordsworth gave him, and thus Shelvocke's miserable voyage resulted at long last in that lovely
mosaic of details from forgotten travel books which is called
The Rime of the Ancient Mariner. The argument of that
poem is the argument of this book: '*How a Ship having passed
the Line was driven by Storm to the cold Country towards the
South Pole; and how from thence she made her course to the
tropical Latitude of the Great Pacific Ocean; and of the strange
things that befell; and in what manner the Ancyent Marinere
came back to his own Country*."

THE BACKGROUND OF THE EIGHTEENTH CENTURY

WE have seen how religious and political problems in Europe in the middle of the seventeenth century left little opportunity for further exploration of the Pacific. The hiatus in actual voyages to that part of the world is mirrored by the absence of those collections of travels which form such a distinctive feature of Tudor and Georgian literature. Between *Hakluytus Posthumus, or Purchas his Pilgrimes* in 1625 and the small collection dedicated to Samuel Pepys in 1694 nothing of the sort was published in this country. The importance of such travel literature is not to be underestimated. Not merely does it provide a source of entertainment and information for posterity, but it illustrates the extent of contemporary interest and affords an immediate inspiration to other voyagers. The first great period of our travel literature is, of course, during the reigns of Elizabeth and James I. The second begins about the time of Anne and continues throughout the century. It is the aim of this chapter to show how the popularity of such books of travel turned the minds of Europeans a second time towards the Pacific, until the mysteries of a still comparatively unknown sea were finally elucidated.

Strictly speaking, the revival of serious interest in the South Seas in this country dates from the publication of the 1694 volume, because in it appeared Narborough's journal and Tasman's "discovery of a New World not yet known to the English." But popular interest was first roused by stories of the buccaneers. Esquemeling's classic *History of the Buccaneers in America* was written before their invasion of the Pacific began; but when it was translated into English in 1684 there appeared, as a supplementary volume, Basil Ringrose's account of the activities of his late comrades in arms there. Indeed, nothing is more extraordinary about that profligate

crew than the number who wrote up their adventures on their
return to this country. Two of their narratives, edited by their
friend Captain Hacke, were presented to the public in 1699.
Many other buccaneers, as well as most of the privateers, kept
journals which they sold to eager publishers; others still remain
unpublished in the collection left by Dr. Sloane to form the
nucleus of the British Museum. As for pirates, Johnson's
*General History of the Robberies and Murders of the Most
Notorious Pyrates* gives a spicy account of their already legendary fame. The boom in the picaresque sea story had begun.

Dampier, of course, stands pre-eminent among such authors.
His first book was published in 1697, and his voyages are collected in the delightful little four-volume edition of 1729.
Unlike the Newgate Calendar style of some of his fellows, or
the dull logs kept by others, his work is that of a scientist who
can write. "It cannot be expected that a Seaman should affect
Politeness," he writes when explaining that he has done his
best for the polite reader to remove uncouth seamanlike ex-
pressions. Whereupon mean-spirited professionals like Defoe
and Swift spread the rumour that he got someone else to write
his books for him. Dampier justly retorted that he only did
what every author did in asking the advice of friends, and there
is no doubt whatever about the honesty of his work.

It is by style a book lives, and it was chiefly on account of his
vigorous style that Dampier won such enormous popularity.
His success is to be measured, not only by the number of editions
his books ran through, but by the imitations which they inspired. Before long, tales of adventure in the South Seas came
to hold the same place for the common reader of Georgian
times as the detective story does today. Professionals were
quick to exploit the new vein. Of course, they affected to
disdain a purely seamanlike style, but they were not past
borrowing whole paragraphs from nautical writers when they
needed colour, as Swift does in Gulliver's first voyage.

However, it was Daniel Defoe, the best liar and the most
industrious journalist of the period, who led the field. Using
Selkirk (whom he does not appear to have met) and other

avellers for copy, he produced that best-seller, *Robinson Crusoe*, in 1719. He quickly followed it up with similar books, such as *Captain Singleton* (based on legends about the pirate Avery), and *A New Voyage Round the World*, a barefaced synthesis of Schouten, Narborough and Dampier.

Swift pretended to despise both Defoe and Dampier, the one because he was not a gentleman and the other because he was a teller of tall stories. He loftily complains that the country is "overstocked with books of travels"; but it is no accident that Gulliver, like Dampier, goes on four voyages, or that the places he visits are all in that conveniently distant part of the world. Lilliput is placed in the middle of Australia, but no geographer of the time was in a position to contradict the author. The land of the Houyhnhnms is a fantasy of the continent which owes a good deal to Dampier. Brobdingnag and Balnibarbi (the slave state of the floating island of Laputa) are somewhere in the north Pacific. The style, the originality of invention, the scarifying satire displayed in these voyages, puts them far apart from the host of imaginary travels which were appearing at that time. Like his modern equivalent in crime, the imaginary traveller strove to be original, but more often than not he was the slave of a formula—the desert island in the South Sea, the shipwrecked mariner, the bold buccaneer, the escaped slave, the happy return. Imaginary captains like Falconer and Boyle, imaginary lands like Psalmanaazar's Formosa, are but reflections of the real thing as described in previous chapters. Turning on his own kind, as was his wont, Swift satirises the craze in his *Project for the Universal Benefit of Mankind*. "The author, having laboured so long, and done so much, to serve and instruct the public, without any advantage to himself, has at last thought of a project which will tend to the great benefit of all mankind, and produce a handsome revenue to the author. He intends to print by subscription, in 96 large volumes in *folio*, an exact description of *Terra Australis Incognita*, collected with great care and pains from 999 learned and pious authors, of undoubted veracity. . . . This work will be of great use for all men, and necessary for all families, because

it contains exact account of all the provinces, colonies an
mansions of that spacious country, where, by a general doom
all transgressors of the law are to be transported."

It cannot be an accident that the year in which those wor₭
appeared (1704) saw the first of the great folio collections whic
go marching down the century: Churchill and Harris an
Moll's huge atlas, down to those of the age of Pinkerton an
Burney, still the best historian of the Pacific. In every case t
central interest is the famous continent.

The way in which the published narratives of voyages in
fluenced public opinion is also illustrated by the host of gimcrac
financial projects which mark the opening of the century. C
these the most famous is the South Sea Company, founded i
1711 (possibly at Defoe's suggestion), and exploding in th
Bubble of 1720. In actual fact it had nothing to do with th
South Seas except in name, for it never sent a ship thither an
it soon became nothing more than a financial ramp; but it
significant that the name itself should be chosen as typifyi
the *El Dorado* of the period. According to Harris, the director
adduced in their defence the profits made by Woodes Roger
"when the plan of it was attacked as insufficient and chimerical.'

The wording of the Act incorporating the Company shoul₫
have put investors on their guard. In the first paragraph ₳
South Sea trade is spoken of as already in existence, but in th₵
third it is explained that it is of the greatest consequence suck
a trade should be established. The area to be exploited con
sisted of the coasts of South America, no ship being permitte₫
to trade outside a belt 300 leagues broad up the west coast, and
no ship was to sail from America to the East Indies. Thus *Terr₵*
Australis lay outside the scope of the project. Meanwhile the
terms of its foundation brushed aside the Spanish claim to ₳
monopoly in those parts. At the end of the War of the Spanish
Succession Spain agreed to hand over the *asiento*, or Atlantic
slave trade, to the Company, but she would not abate one jo₮
of her ancient pretensions in the Pacific.

In 1720 there occurred a similar financial slump in France.
This was chiefly due to the collapse of John Law's *Compagnie*

es Indes, which also promised a monopoly in those parts. The rench had at least begun to lay the foundations of a trade there, ut, once financial interests were allowed to interfere, it collapsed in the same catastrophic way as the English company. y the end of the year, thousands of ruined speculators in both ountries had reason to curse the fatal attraction of the South as.

The revival of political interest in the Pacific was due to the ossibility of the unwieldy empire of Spain breaking up when he death of Charles II in 1700 precipitated the War of the panish Succession. Such hopes were dashed by the special ause in the Treaty of Utrecht at the end of the war which asserted Spanish claims in that ocean. Nevertheless farghted individuals continued to press upon their Governments he importance of expansion in the southern hemisphere. As as Holland was concerned, the advice of Purry to colonise ustralia, and the voyage of Roggeveen to discover the southern ntinent, came to nothing. In England and France more efinite steps were taken. Both countries had their paper South ea companies; both had their privateers and buccaneers; oth had their semi-official spies to see what prospect there was or trade. At home, geographers and projectors clamoured for enewed attempts to solve the mystery.

The English buccaneers with whom we were concerned in he last chapter were by no means the only ones in the Pacific. There were numerous brushes between men like Dampier and heir French rivals, for though French corsairs appeared in those eas a few years later than the English, when they came, they ame in greater numbers. Between 1695 and 1726 over one undred voyages to Peru are recorded; of these eleven continued round the world, though little is known about them. The first expedition was led by an ex-naval captain named De Gennes, and was backed by important personages, but t never reached the Pacific. The aim of the next expedition, under Beauchesne, was chiefly to remedy the defect to which the failure of the first was due: lack of accurate knowledge about the entry into the unknown sea. Beauchesne sailed

with royal authority to spend seven months charting the entries
but, like Narborough, he met with a cool reception when h
reached South American waters.   On the outbreak of wa
however, accredited privateers were made more welcome, sinc
the nominal King of Spain was now Louis XIV's grandson an
their services could be enlisted against the English rovers.

In 1701 two St. Malo ships under Pierre Perrée du Coudra
later Sieur de Villestrau.... turned with a cargo worth 160,0(
livres.   His success popularised the trade.   A *Compagnie de l
Chine de Saint Malo* was formed, and many adventurers mac
a fortune by following his tracks.   As the war continued an
the Spanish colonies became isolated from their normal source (
supply, the trade became immensely profitable: cargoes wor
7 million *livres*, 30 million *livres* began to be reported.   (
course only a minute proportion ever reached the royal treasury
but imagine the joy at Versailles over something that really di
pay a profit!   One authority estimates that between 1707 an
1720 250 million *livres* reached France in this way.

The geographical knowledge thus acquired proved of grea
value to later explorers.   It was these men who named what th
Dutch called the Sebaldines, and the English the Falklands
Les Malouines and established the first settlement there at Por
Louis.   One of their number discovered what he called th
Passage de St. Barbe, between Tierra del Fuego and the island
farther west.   Another observed more exactly the position o
the Horn and the trend of the coast north, so that eighteentl
century maps of South America cease to have the stuntec
appearance which they have in atlases of the previous century.

The most important voyage of all was the official expeditior
led by Frézier in 1711-1714.   His instructions were "to mak
Hydrographical observations for the use of mariners and for the
correction of charts," as well as to find out the position o
Spanish strong points, the possibilities of trade, the habits o
the natives, etc.   Though he sailed as a trader in a merchan
ship, he was really nothing more than a government spy.   His
work is a notable contribution to the topography of this region.
The surprising thing is that its publication was permitted, with

he result that it was promptly translated into English, with a
edication to the Prince of Wales as the Governor of the South
ea Company. The translator hoped that it would prove useful
> the company; actually it served for a guidebook to men of
he stamp of Shelvocke, who frequently refers to it.   As to
Terra Australis, Frézier says "those Southern Lands generally
aid down in the old charts are mere chimeras, which have
astly been left out of the new charts"; but a glance at one of
he atlases published at the time is not reassuring.   In the
mappemonde of M. Delisle, for example, shreds of the southern
ontinent still hang about the bottom of the map; New Guinea
s still joined to Australia; there is evidence of a North-West
assage; and the Solomons have by now migrated half-way
cross the ocean.

The lust for gold and that curiosity which impels men to see
hat lies around the corner have always been the predomin-
ing motives of exploration. Usually both are present, but as
he eighteenth century advances the magic word "gold" falls
ut of use in favour of politer words such as "trade" or "colon-
sation"; at the same time, in these state-aided expeditions,
uriosity and the love of adventure take on a more scientific
one. The turning point between the old period of privileged
lunderers and the new period of official scientific exploration
s Anson's voyage of 1740-1744.

This famous circumnavigation belongs in strategy and out-
ine to the Elizabethan pattern. It was the last of the type.
Henceforward, in naval warfare, predatory expeditions such as
his gives place to a strategy pivoting on the blockade of Brest
y a Western Squadron. When it was realised how negligible
were the effects of this voyage upon the course of the War of
he Austrian Succession a sounder strategy, on the base of
vhich British naval supremacy was built, was adopted, the man
hiefly responsible for the change being Anson himself. Nor
vas his voyage important as far as geographical exploration was
oncerned, for he followed the well-known route—St. Julian,
he Horn, Payta, the Mexican coast, the Marianas. Thence the
Centurion made her way to the Canton river, being the first

British warship to visit China. As the result of intercepting th
Manila galleon near the Philippines, £480,000 worth of treasur
was taken; but the cost in terms of human life was very heav

The consequences rather than the course of the voyage co
cern us here. In the first place, it is the classic example of th
deadly effects of scurvy. Before the introduction of canne
provisions and the frigidaire, a diet composed exclusively of sa
meat and biscuit, washed down with rum, resulted in a deficienc
of vitamin C, the vitamin found in fresh vegetables. Immunit
to diseases like scurvy and dysentery was further weakened k
low standards of cleanliness and living conditions. Scurvy itse
affected sailors in different ways: pains in the joints; a swellin
of the gums; hæmorrhages; brittle bones; an extraordina
lassitude, combined with an access of low spirits. "A strang
dejection of spirits, with shivering, tremblings, and a dispositio
to be seized with the most dreadful terrors on the slighte
accident," notes one of the narrators of Anson's voyage. "Mar
of our people though confined to their hammocks, were cheerfu
and talked, with seeming vigour in a loud, strong voice; ye
on their being in the least moved, though it was only from or
part of the ship to another, and that, too, in their hammock
they have immediately expired. Others who, confiding in the
seeming strength, have resolved to get out of their hammock
have died before they could reach the deck." The mere sme
and touch of mother earth seems to have revived some; othe
pathetically lay about the decks, rolling from side to side wit
the motion of the ship, until they were swept overboard.

Every long voyage was marked by a recurrence of th
disease, but on some voyages it was worse than others. Any
body who took the trouble to study the incidence of the diseas
(and the naval authorities were the last people to do so), coul
say definitely that the longer the voyage, the more certain wa
scurvy; the dirtier the ship, the more exhausted the men, th
greater the number of deaths. The chief lesson to be learne
from Anson's experience was that overcrowding was fata
The statistics collected by Vice-Admiral Boyle Somerville in hi
excellent account of the voyage put this beyond questio

aturally the 500 decrepit Chelsea pensioners, which a crimin-
lly stupid administration sent to sea, never stood a chance of
vithstanding the rigours of a long Pacific voyage. But hardly
single officer died. In the *Anna* pink of 400 tons, with a crew
f 16, not one died from scurvy. In the *Tryall* of 200 tons, 57
ut of 96 men died before reaching Juan Fernandez. While in
ae *Gloucester* which carried a number of soldiers, 278 out of
96 died. Out of the 1955 men who sailed from England in
 ships, 1051 died from scurvy. Only 145 returned in the
enturion, the one ship which succeeded in sailing round the
vorld. Pizarro's squadron, which was sent out to intercept
nson, seems to have suffered even worse: only 100 out of
000 Spaniards ever returned.

   In the face of such catastrophic losses one asks why, if the
isease was so well known, had nothing been done about it?
omething had, outside the Navy. East Indiamen, for example,
ere generally known as "lime-juicers" (possibly the origin of
 e American word "limey"), on account of their issue of lime
uice. This appears to have been a misnomer, for it is the lemon
nd not the West Indian lime which possesses the requisite anti-
corbutic properties. As early as 1634 Captain Boteler describes
t as "excellent against the scorbute." Every seaman knew
he value of fresh vegetables, and good commanders made use
f the islands they touched at to collect a supply. But islands
re not common in the north Pacific. The only medicine provided for Anson and his men was a violent purgative called "the
'ill and Drop of Dr. Ward." Moreover, the worst casualties
occurred before he ever reached the Pacific proper, on account
f overcrowding and the exhausted state of his men resulting
rom a singularly difficult passage round the Horn. The correct
liagnosis of the disease begins, not with Cook, as popular legend
1as it, but with Dr. James Lind's treatise on the subject in 1753,
1is researches being inspired by what Anson's men had suffered.
n spite of the example set by Cook and his contemporary, Sir
Gilbert Blane (principal medical officer in Rodney's fleet during
he American war), lemon juice was not officially issued to all
I.M. ships until the very end of the century.

H

Anson's disastrous passage round the Horn leads us to second aspect of this voyage. So little progress had been mad in the art of navigation since the time of the first explorers tha the master's mate on board the flagship was capable of makin an error of 9° in his estimated longitude, in consequence o which the ships turned north too soon after passing Cape Horn In the darkness the signal gun of the leading ship gave warnin of breakers ahead; the squadron was 350 miles to the east o the estimated position, and Anson had to turn his ships sout again to avoid the rocky cliffs of Cape Noir. More gales, eve increasing in fury, had to be fought to increase his westing, s that scores of exhausted men fell a prey to scurvy in consequenc of a navigational error. At least 70 more died on board th *Centurion* because, even when they reached the latitude Juan Fernandez, their ignorance of longitude was such tha they spent eleven days finding out if they were east or west o the island. The men of the *Gloucester* were so weak that sh took no less than fourteen days to reach her anchorage aft sighting it. As for the *Severn*, her captain declared on he return that when he thought he was steering for the rendezvou in Chile he found himself off the coast of Patagonia on th opposite side of the continent.

These incredible facts were solely due to the absence o chronometers. Here again the century saw a notable advance but the invention was adopted too late to benefit any of th voyagers whose exploits are recorded in this volume. Othe countries had offered prizes for an efficient marine timekeepe before the English did so in 1714 (shortly after the Board o Longitude had been established at Greenwich). John Harriso ultimately won the prize, or part of it, for the Board was mea enough to deny him the full sum. His first timekeeper wa tested on board the *Centurion* in 1736, but it was not regarde as sufficiently accurate to be taken with her round the world The first commander to do so was Cook, who carried the prize winning watch with him in 1772 on his second voyage an found it "our faithful guide." Thus none of his predecessor possessed the means of determining their position accurately

and none of them had the benefits of medical knowledge which
would have diminished the casualties they suffered on account
of the errors in navigation they inevitably made.

Another thing that the voyage made clear was the necessity
of a southern base. During Anson's long tenure of office at the
Admiralty he was fully alive to this need. The much maligned
Sandwich was a member of the Board during most of that time,
and it was probably due to his contact with Anson that, when
the semi-official voyages to the Pacific began, their secondary
objective was invariably the reconnaissance of a base, either in
the Falklands, or at Juan Fernandez, or somewhere on the coast
of Chile.

Next to *Robinson Crusoe*, accounts of Anson's voyage achieved
more international popularity than any other book of travel of
the period. The description of island paradises, such as Tinian
in the Marianas, must have had a good deal to do with the vogue
of the myth of the Noble Savage and the State of Nature. At
this date Rousseau was just beginning his attack on the dangers
of civilisation, and it is said that his disciple, Bernardin de
St. Pierre, knew his *Robinson Crusoe* off by heart. To such
readers nothing could be more romantic than the description of
the pleasure with which Anson's scurvy-ridden crew viewed the
green lawns of Tinian, where herds of milk-white cattle grazed
beneath fruit-bearing trees. Well might the poor wretches
have exclaimed with Marvel—

> What wondrous life is this I lead!
> Ripe apples drop about my head;
> The luscious clusters of the vine
> Upon my mouth do crush their wine;
> The nectarine and curious peach
> Into my hands themselves do reach;
> Stumbling on melons, as I pass,
> Insnared with flowers, I fall on grass.

All of which was nearly literally true, if guavas and oranges are
substituted for the nectarine and curious peach.

The year Anson returned to this country a certain John
Campbell began to issue a new edition of Harris' collection of

voyages. It is to monumental collections such as this that we must turn if we wish to see the background against which the last stage of Pacific exploration was carried out. In these huge volumes lie the seed of the final discoveries. The patriotic Campbell addressed his book to the "Merchants of Great Britain" in an attempt to convince them of riches as yet undiscovered. To do this he had to touch up the depressing picture of Australia drawn by earlier visitors, though the known facts did not in the least warrant his optimism. None the less it is fascinating to see how he anticipated the discovery of rich gold-fields in Australia and the strategic importance of New Britain. He advised his countrymen to lose no time in appropriating countries which the Dutch had failed to exploit. As to Terra Australis (which he imagined to lie farther east), he urged that its position at least should be finally fixed: its western seaboard was no doubt Tasman's New Zealand, and its northern promontories had been seen by men like Quiros and Schouten and Roggeveen. To this end, the Falklands and Juan Fernandez were the obvious bases.

Meanwhile French opinion was moving in the same direction. Distinguished *philosophes* like Buffon, the naturalist, and Maupertuis, the mathematician, were saying much the same thing at the same time. In the forefront of the programme of the Academy of Science, over which Maupertuis presided, was a project for the discovery of *Terra Australis*, and the most important French work on the subject grew out of a paper read to one of its discussion groups.

This was the two-volume work of Charles de Brosses, President of the *Parlement* of Burgundy, which appeared in 1756. Its title gives the scope of its contents: "*Histoire des Navigations aux Terres Australes, contenant ce que l'on sçait des mœurs et des productions des Contrées découvertes jusqu'à ce jour; et où il est traité de l'utilité d'y faire de plus amples découvertes, et des moyens d'y former un établissement.*" Lytton Strachey has given us a delightful portrait in miniature of the only man to get the better of Voltaire, and whom he in revenge prevented from becoming a member of the Academy. As the first of distinguished band of French archaeologists and anthropologists, De Brosses richly deserved a seat. The work under discussion was by far the most original and scientific approach to the problem of the Pacific which had hitherto appeared. Writing on the eve of the Seven Years War, he warned his countrymen that "a neighbouring power is aiming at the universal monarchy of the seas," and that unless France acted quickly the richest prize—*Terra Australis*—would fall into British hands. Instead of aiming at the conquest of some wretched ravaged province, of two or three cannon-shattered fortresses, the discovery of such a continent would be "the grandest, noblest, most useful enterprise a sovereign could undertake." It was not necessary to conquer it in the ruthless Spanish manner, but rather to establish forts and factories on its coasts, as the Dutch had done in Africa, whence the seeds of French civilisation would spread amongst its benighted inhabitants. As the first step, some island like Juan Fernandez must be occupied. We shall see how Louis XV, after his discomfiture in the Seven Years War, acted on this advice.

The *Terres Australes*, as De Brosses understands them, are not one continent, but a collection of huge islands which maintain the equilibrium of the globe. He neatly divides these territories into three parts, inventing the names which we still use for those parts which really do exist. Everything lying to the south of Asia he calls Australasia; the lands he imagined to lie in the South Atlantic he calls Magellanica; while to "everything which the vast pacific ocean contains, I shall give the name *Polynesia* on account of the number of islands to be found there." Proceeding to a detailed description, he estimates that the territories cover an area of eight to ten million square miles, with a proportionately huge population. The potential value of the fruits, minerals, fish, etc., to be found there staggers even his imagination. In order to stake out a prior claim to the southern lands he cites the legendary voyage of the Sieur de Gonneville in 1503. (Actually Gonneville discovered Madagascar, or it may have been Brazil.) In these days, he concludes, an overseas empire is the destiny of great nations. "One cannot

too frequently repeat in France, that he who is master of the
sea is master of the land."

There were those in France, notably the Duc de Choiseul
and M. de Bougainville, who heeded his words. The French
Empire in the Pacific is what remains of his dream. The outcome of the Seven Years War decided which nation was to win
the prize of empire, and it is significant that when an un-
acknowledged translation of his work appeared in England at
the end of the war his translator, John Callandar, was in a
position to brag of the might of his country at the expense of
defeated rival.. "United among ourselves, respected by foreign-
ers, with our marine force entire, and (humanly speaking)
invincible, aided by a set of naval officers superior in every
respect to those of the nations around us, etc., etc. . . ." With
even more assurance than the man whose argument he plagiar-
ises, Callandar entitled his work *Terra Australis Cognita*, for
"these seas are known, the latitude and longitude of the principal lands are ascertained." Who could doubt it?

This was the question to which the final group of Pacific
explorers attempted to find an answer. We must imagine them
as setting out, as so many had done before them, to sail beyond
the sunset for a prize painted for them in glittering colours by
geographers at home. Unlike the first lonely wanderers, they
had behind them, not only the newly awakened interest of a
wide public, but the prestige of great powers brought to the
edge of conflict by their rivalry to find and claim that which had
remained hidden for so long. The stage was set for the last act.

VIII

FOUL WEATHER JACK

AT half-past four in the morning of May 14, 1741, His Majesty's ship *Wager* struck the rocks of a barren island 90 leagues north of the western exit of the Straits of Magellan. She had lost touch with the other ships of Commodore Anson's squadron in the gales encountered off the Horn, and her loss was particularly serious since she carried most of the equipment for the intended landings in South America. Like the other ships, she was manned by a pressed crew and "a poor detachment of decrepit and inferior invalids from Chelsea Hospital." One of the three midshipmen on board was the Hon. John Byron, grandfather of the poet. This was his first encounter with the sort of weather which he was destined to meet in every one of the seven seas, earning him his service nickname of Foul Weather Jack.

The wreck of the *Wager* was a terrible initiation to the South Seas. As soon as the ship struck on the fangs of that desolate coast all semblance of discipline vanished. Anyone who could move immediately rushed on deck, leaving those victims of scurvy who were confined to their hammocks to be drowned below. Those of the sick who succeeded in reaching the deck were many of them so weak that they were washed overboard by the waves sweeping over the ship. Some went mad with fear, falling on their knees and praying for mercy, or jumping over the side into the boiling surf. One poor fellow rushed about waving a cutlass calling himself the King of the Country and cutting down everyone within reach, until somebody knocked him overboard. Few kept their heads beside the helmsman, who stuck to his post though rudder and tiller were gone, and the mate, who did his best to recall the men to a sense of their duty. In vain, for the ship was breaking up under them as the seas pounded her upon the rocks.

When the clouds lifted they could discern the snowy peaks

of the Cordilleras rising to the east beyond the rocky island
The officers put off in the barges and yawl to establish a camp
on shore. That was the signal for pandemonium to break out
among those left behind in the ship. Led by the bo'sun, the
men rushed below, staving in casks and chests, wantonly smash-
ing everything they could find. Many were soon so drunk that
they reeled across the sloping deck into the sea. When the
bo'sun thought fit to recall a boat to take them off, he fired two
shots from the quarter-deck gun directly at the Indian hove
where the Captain had established himself. In obedience to th...
summons, the latter came on board, found the men dressed up in
officers' finery rifled from below, and knocked their leader down

It was unfortunate that at the time of the wreck Captain
Cheap had dislocated his shoulder. At the best of times he ha
nothing to commend him save his courage. But from the
moment the ship struck he showed himself utterly incompetent
to maintain discipline in the face of the catastrophe which had
befallen him. A hundred and forty men were saved from the
wreck, but the number was soon reduced by a third in consequence of the murdering and pillaging on shore. Whatever
the Captain could do, the store tent was robbed daily. Two
marine culprits were sentenced to 600 lashes each; 200 were
given them, but the ravenous crew demanded their instant death.
Starvation soon reached such a point that a ship's boy was with
difficulty restrained from eating the liver of a drowned sailor.

The problem of maintaining any semblance of order was
complicated by the fact that in those days a captain's authority
ceased with the disappearance of his ship. In consequence of
Cheap's experience the law was changed, but his behaviour was
such that he could never have won the loyalty of his men, even
if the law had been on his side. The event which precipitated
what we should call a mutiny was his inhuman treatment of a
midshipman named Cozens, recently promoted from the lower
deck and extremely popular with the men. Cozens was rolling
a cask of brandy up to the store tent. Finding it heavy for him,
he paused to straighten his back. At that moment the Captain
appeared.

"You're drunk!" he shouted.

"With what should I get drunk, unless it be with water?" replied Cozens.

"You scoundrel, get more hands and roll the cask up," answered Cheap, striking him with his cane. Cozens muttered something about Shelvocke to the disparagement of the Captain. "Tho' Shelvocke was a rogue he was no fool; and by God you are both!" shouted Cheap. He then attempted to strike Cozens again, but was prevented by a bystander.

Two days later Cozens quarrelled with the purser, in the course of which he attempted to shoot him, and would have done so had not the pistol been knocked out of his hand. Emerging from his tent at the sound of the shot, Cheap ran up and, without so much as asking a question, shot Cozens through the jaw. The boy was not dead, but Cheap refused to allow anyone to attend him, in consequence of which he died after lying weltering in his blood for some days.

The Captain's headstrong behaviour on this occasion profoundly shocked the crew. At the same time a scheme was being propounded of which Cheap totally disapproved. Mr. Bulkeley, the gunner, a man of a strong and independent mind, came across young Byron reading the narrative of Sir John Narborough, which had somehow been saved from the wreck. Looking at the plan of the Straits which the volume contained, the idea occurred to him that the best way out of their present predicament was to return through the Straits in the ship's boats. Several of the officers agreed with him, but when it was suggested to the Captain the latter strongly opposed it, though he was unwise enough not to admit this openly. The idea of an open boat journey like that seemed to him to be crazy. His suggestion was that they should make for the rendezvous at Socorro to the northward; failing that, that they should give themselves up at the nearest Spanish settlement, which he mistakenly imagined to be not far off. The discussion dragged on for several weeks, the men becoming increasingly exasperated by hunger and Cheap's temporisations.

On October 9 Captain Pemberton of the marines made the

decisive move. Accompanied by a body of supporters, he surprised Cheap in his tent in bed.

"What are you about? Where are my officers?" shouted
the Captain. The gunner and others coming in, he repeated the
question, "Gentlemen, do you know what you are about?"

"Yes, sir; our assistance was demanded by Captain Pemberton to secure you as a prisoner for the death of Mr. Cozens."

"Gentlemen," replied Cheap, "Captain Pemberton has
nothing to do with me; I am your commander still; I will
show you my Instructions." As they refused to be impressed
he gave up. "Gentlemen, you have caught me napping; I do
not see any of you in liquor; you are a parcel of brave fellows
but my officers are scoundrels."

He asked Lieutenant Beans what he proposed to do with him.
Beans replied that he was to be put under guard in the purser's
tent. "Hum!" says the Captain, "I should be obliged to the
gentlemen if they would let me stay in my own tent." His
request was refused. "Well, gentlemen, you must excuse my
not pulling my hat off, my hands are confined." Turning to the
lieutenant, he said ironically, "Well, *Captain* Beans, you will
be called to an account for this hereafter." As they marched
him off the bo'sun struck him in the face, saying "Then it was
your time; but now, God damn you, it is mine!" With some
dignity Cheap replied, "You are a scoundrel for using a gentleman ill when he is a prisoner."

Four days later the mutineers made ready the cutter and the
longboat, which they christened the *Speedwell*. Leaving Cheap
and a handful of officers with meagre provisions, 81 of them
made sail to the southward, taking Byron with them. However,
he and a few others took an early opportunity to slip back in
the cutter to rejoin the marooned party.

The voyage of the *Speedwell*, while not so famous as Bligh's
later exploit, is one of the most remarkable open boat journeys
on record. With nothing but the assistance of Narborough's
old chart, they made the passage through the Straits and up the
coast of Patagonia to Montevideo in four months. Only thirty
men got there alive, for almost daily Bulkeley records the death

of one or more of their number, first the boys and then the older men. The cook, however, aged 82, lasted until they were within sight of safety. Entries like this are frequent—

"The Night departed this Life Mr. Thomas Caple, Son of the late Lieutenant Caple, aged twelve Years, who perish'd for want of Food. . . .

"The 6th died Thomas Harvey, the Purser. This Gentleman died a mere Skeleton for want of Food, and was probably the first Purser, belonging to His Majesty's Service, that ever perish'd with Hunger."

Some of the more fortunate secured a passage back to Europe in January 1743. The first news they heard in England was that their late captain was a prisoner in Chile. Since, in the eyes of the law, they were not mutineers, and since Bulkeley had kept a journal in which he was careful to take every legal precaution, he and the others were permitted to go to their homes and the case was suspended until the return of their officers.

Captain Cheap, Lieutenant Hamilton and Midshipmen Byron and Campbell were the only survivors of the score of men originally marooned on Wager Island. They reached a Spanish prison after a journey of unparalleled hardships which are described in Byron's *Narrative of the Loss of the Wager*, published over twenty years after Bulkeley's narrative appeared. As one of the best tales of adventure ever written, it deserves to be better known than it is.

Before they were driven north by hunger they were all of them seriously ill in consequence of what Byron calls "the vile stuff I eat"—mussels, limpets, sea-urchins, herbs and dead dogs bought off visiting Indians. Their first journey in the barge and yawl lasted two months and brought them back to their starting point, Mount Misery; they had even eaten the shoes off their feet. Some Indians then took them off with the intention of handing them over to the Spaniards. Cheap's selfishness increased with his illness. His clothes were so crawling with vermin that he looked, says Byron, like an ant hill and his beard was as long as a hermit's. But as leader of the party he was

treated better than the others, for whom he showed no con
sideration whatever. He allowed the Indians to treat the mid
shipmen like slaves, not even permitting them to share a fir
or lie under cover after pulling all day. He even refused to giv
an exhausted man a piece of seal's meat when the latter collapse
under the thwart of the boat.

A year after the wreck Byron describes his own appearanc
as follows: "What we suffered at this time is not easily to b
expressed. I had been three days at the oar without any kin
of nourishment, but the wretched root I mentioned before.
had no shirt, as mine was rotted off by bits; and we wer
devoured by vermin. All my cloaths consisted of an old shor
grieko, which is something like a bear-skin, with a piece of
waistcoat under it, which had once been of red cloth, both whicl
I had on when I was cast away; I had a ragged pair of trousers
without either shoes or stockings. . . . After working like
galley slave all day, toward night, when we landed, instead o
taking any rest, Mr. Campbell and I were sometimes obliged t
go miles along shore to get a few shell fish; and just as we hav
made a little fire in order to dress them, he (the Indian) ha
commanded us into the boat again, and kept us rowing the whol
night without ever landing."

Before they reached the nearest Spanish settlement the
were handed over to a more friendly tribe which took them t
the island of Chiloe. The first European they met was a Jesuit
Seeing the Captain produce a gold watch (heaven knows how
he had preserved it), "the first thing the good father did was t
lug out of his pocket a bottle of brandy, and give us a dram, in
order to open our hearts. He then came roundly to the point,
asking if we had saved no watches or rings." Upon which Cheap
ordered Campbell to hand over his silver watch. The Jesuit at
least took them to prison, where Byron filled his belly for the
first time in thirteen months.

The two midshipmen made a rapid recovery and were soon
allowed to live on parole with an old lady. Young Byron won
many hearts with his handsome looks and romantic story. A
priest's niece even expressed her willingness to marry him, but

before matters reached such a conclusion the annual ship called
to transfer the prisoners to the mainland. Thence a St. Malo
ship took them back to France, narrowly escaping capture at the
hands of British cruisers. Though the War of the Austrian
Succession was still in progress, they were permitted to find their
way back to England. In the autumn of 1745 young Byron
reached his sister's house in Soho to find the capital in a state of
alarm on account of the Jacobite invasion, and to hear news of
the return of the mutineers and of the Commodore himself.
He was at sea again in command of a sloop the next year.

The dominant theme of international affairs in the eight-
enth century was the colonial rivalry between France and
Britain. Successive wars were merely continuations of that
policy by other means. The Atlantic and Indian oceans were
the chief theatres, but after the conclusion of the Seven Years
War the Pacific became the scene of a more peaceful, and hence
a more neglected, rivalry. The point at issue was not only the
discovery of the long-sought continent, but the possession of a
base from which to pursue such discoveries either to the east
or to the west. The Falkland Islands off the coast of Patagonia
seemed to be cast by nature for this part in the drama. No
wonder that another European war nearly broke out over the
question of their control ten years after the conclusion of the
Peace of Paris in 1763.

The British, on Anson's recommendation, had made the first
move as far back as 1749, when our ambassador at Madrid
informed the Spanish government that the Admiralty proposed
to send a ship for "the full discovery of Pepys and Falkland
Islands; . . . there is no intention of making any settlement in
either of these islands." Strange to say, the innocence of these
intentions was misunderstood, so, to calm the ruffled feelings
of the Spanish Government, the matter was dropped for the
time being.

It was revived as soon as the Seven Years War was over, and
the man chosen to carry it out was John Byron. Apart from
having suffered shipwreck at the entrance into the South Sea
at the age of seventeen, and having proved himself a competent

commander of a line-of-battle ship in the late war, it is difficul
to see exactly what were his qualifications for the task. However, the Admiralty meant business, for Byron's ship wa:
exceptionally well fitted out, in contrast to his previous experience. She was the *Dolphin*, a sixth rate mounting 24 guns,
with a crew of 150 men, 3 lieutenants and 37 petty officers;
though not actually the first copper-bottomed vessel, she was
the first to be fitted with copper braces and pintles to her rudder.
She carried a "machine" for distilling water, "fearnough
jackets" for high latitudes, and plenty of "portable soup," th
latest specific against scurvy. Her consort was the *Tamar* sloo
of 16 guns and a crew of 113 commanded by Captain Mouat
with Philip Carteret as first lieutenant. A storeship was sen
out to meet them off South America.

When matters of high diplomacy are involved, published
aims are seldom explicit. So, when the two ships sailed and the
Commodore hoisted his pennant as Commander-in-Chief, East
Indies, it was generally supposed that such was their destination.
But Byron's Secret Orders, preserved in the Public Record
Office, show that the real objective was very different. It is
interesting to note the strong Elizabethan flavour about them,
showing whence the inspiration came for this second great age
of discovery. In the preamble Byron is ordered to search for
any islands, such as Pepys and the Falklands, "unvisited by any
European power (which) may be found in the Atlantick Ocean
between the Cape of Good Hope and the Magellanick Streights,
within Latitudes convenient for navigation and in the Climates
adapted to the Produce of Commodities usefull in Commerce."
After that he was to examine New Albion, unvisited since the
days of Drake, and, like him, to search for a Pacific entrance to
a North-West Passage between latitudes 39° and 54° N. (Parlia-
ment had recently revived this old quest by offering a prize of
£20,000.) You are in consequence, the Orders continue, to
proceed to Brazil; thence stretch across to the Cape, and having
provisioned there to work back in a westerly direction in search
of Pepys Island in 47° or 48° S., "stretching occasionally in your
way thither as far to the Southward as the Latitude of 53°, and

searching diligently for any Land or Islands that may be situated
between the Cape of Good Hope and Pepys Island within the
Latitudes of 33° and 53° South."

It then appears to have occurred to Their Lordships that this
course might not be possible in the South Atlantic in the latitude
of the Roaring Forties, so Byron is given the option, if he
thought the season was too advanced when he left Rio, to
proceed first to Pepys Island. "Having done so you are to
proceed Southward to His Majesty's Islands called Falkland
Islands, which are described to lie between the Lats. of 50° 00'
nd 53° 00' South, about the same distance from the Continent
s Pepys Island: And having made the like Surveys at those
Islands you are to proceed Three Hundred Leagues to the Eastward between the Lats. of 33° 00' and 53° 00' South in order
to make discovery of any Lands or Islands that may be situated
between these Latitudes."

After taking possession, he was to winter at Pepys Island—
presumably at Cowley's famous harbour which would accommodate a thousand ships—where the *Florida* storeship would
await him. In the event (which they appear to have thought
unlikely) of the anchorage being unsuitable, they were to meet
at Port Desire on the coast of Patagonia, where search was to
be made for any possible survivors of the *Wager*. When the
season permitted he was to proceed west in search of New
Albion. If he could not find a passage back via Hudson Bay, he
was "to proceed to the Coast of Asia" and so home. Then
comes the final proviso, of which Byron took full advantage:

But forasmuch in an undertaking of this important Nature
several Emergencies may arise, not to be foreseen, and therefore not to be provided for by Instructions beforehand, you
are, in all cases, to proceed as you shall judge may be most
advantageous to the Service on which you are employed.

Given under our hands the 17th of June, 1764.

Egmont
Carysfort
Howe.

Four days later the *Dolphin* and *Tamar* sailed from the
Downs.   At Rio the Commodore met Clive on his way out
to India in a slow East Indiaman.   He begged Byron to
take him on board and give him a quicker passage.   What
reason Byron gave for refusing him this service we shall never
know.

On October 20, they weighed and made sail from Rio in the
direction of the Cape of Good Hope.   Two days later a signal was
made for the Captain of the *Tamar* to come on board, and all
hands were piped on deck.   To everyone's surprise the Commodore announced that they were bound for the South Seas.
The secret had been so well kept that the men had sold all their
warm clothing, so new slops were issued.   When it was announced that by order of Their Lordships every man was to
receive double pay, "they all expressed the greatest joy imagin-
able"; and when, a few weeks later, the storeship was sent
home and anyone who wished to take a passage in her was
permitted to do so, only one man took advantage of the offer.
If Foul Weather Jack was unlucky in the weather, he was
fortunate in the men and the ship he commanded; nor was it
merely a question of luck, for at every crisis he showed himself
most considerate as a leader of men.

So far the weather had been perfect, but as they ran south
they were so buffeted by storms that they were glad to struggle
into the anchorage at Port Desire.   Here they found one of those
odd mementoes which are always cropping up as one explorer
follows another: a broken musket "with the King's broad arrow
upon it," probably from the *Sweepstakes* or the *Speedwell*.
Having refreshed themselves they made sail in search of their
first objective: Pepys Island.   It did not take Byron long to
decide that there was no such place.   Indeed, his search for it
was so perfunctory that it is obvious, even at this stage of the
voyage, that he had not got the temperament of the true
explorer.   Not for him the tacking to and fro, the lying-to at
night, the sedulous care with which clues of land are followed
up.   He did what he had to do as quickly as possible, taking
advantage of every loophole his instructions afforded to push on

vith all speed, ever anxious to avoid the calamities which
aunted him from his knowledge of Anson's experiences.

They returned to sight the opening of the Magellan Straits
oon after Christmas (midsummer, if such a name can be given
o the wan sunlight of those desolate regions). In consequence
f traffic with the Patagonians, the old story of their gigantic
ize receives what appears to be remarkable confirmation. Byron
imself was six feet tall, but he says of the chief of these "enormous goblins" that, though "I did not measure him, if I may
udge of his height by the proportion of his stature to my own,
could not be less than seven feet." His first lieutenant was
x feet two, but when the chief patted him familiarly on the
ack, "it affected his whole frame." Of course this story made
tremendous stir on their return. "The nation of Brobding-
ags" had at last been found, according to Horace Walpole.

Soon after the New Year orders were given to weigh and set
n easterly course for the Falklands, of which English seamen
ad still only the vaguest idea. Byron made his landfall on the
vestern side near a magnificent bay, one of the finest natural
arbours in the world, where "the whole navy of England
night ride in perfect security from all winds." Port Egmont
e called it, in honour of the First Lord of the day. The sur-
ounding country was bleak and treeless, but birds abounded,
o that the deck soon looked like a poulterer's shop. The object
eing merely to survey the place, no settlement was made, but
3yron took possession in the name of His Majesty with such
eremony as the occasion permitted, his men making "very
nerry, a large bowl of arrack punch being carried on shore,
ut of which they drank several loyal toasts."

After a short stay he coasted round the north of the island,
trewing English names along the bays and headlands, and
urveying the coast in his perfunctory fashion. Indeed, when
e opened a great bay on the eastern side of the island he did
ot so much as trouble to sail into it. Had he done so, he would
ave found that a flourishing French settlement had been
stablished at the head of it for the past nine months. On
eturning to the Straits he sent home the *Florida* with a despatch

announcing what he had done. So the first step in the Falkland dispute was made, with representatives of each nation taking possession in perfect ignorance of each other's existence in the locality.

Yet when Byron re-entered the Straits in February some inkling of what was happening may have crossed his mind. A strange sail was sighted, which he at first took to be a Spanish man-of-war. Preparations were made to give her a warm reception, but darkness fell before they closed. Next day she was seen following the *Dolphin* at a distance, and even put out boats to go to the assistance of one of the English ships which had taken the ground. Boats from the *Dolphin* anticipated them, and it was found that the ship was French, but her name and business could not be ascertained. When the *Dolphin* and *Tamar* resumed their course they left the stranger anchored in a cove. Not till many years later did Byron learn that she was the *Aigle*, with Bougainville on board, bringing stores to his colonists on his second visit to the Falklands.

With all its discomforts, and with only Narborough's old chart and Bulkeley's observations to guide him, Byron was convinced that the passage of the Straits was preferable to that of the Horn. Here were at least achorages like Port Famine, which belied the name Cavendish had given it, in so far as it offered an opportunity to take on wood and water. If the passage was made about Christmas time, Byron reckoned that it ought not to take more than three weeks. He himself took 42 days from Port Famine to Cape Pillar, a distance of about 200 miles as the crow flies, but involving a thousand tacks on account of head winds. Two years later Wallis took his advice, but had to spend over four months in the Straits, though his ship was also the *Dolphin*.

Issuing from the Straits on April 9, 1765, he met the full force of the westerly gales, just the sort which had wrecked the *Wager* hereabouts a quarter of a century earlier. We can imagine with what feelings of anxiety he struggled on to Masafuera, near Juan Fernandez. He succeeded in reaching it and what is more, the *Tamar* was still in company and there was little sign of scurvy. Compared with Anson, he thought himself immensely fortunate. Here he made several changes among his officers: Mouat and Carteret were transferred to the *Dolphin* as Captain and First Lieutenant; Cummings, the first lieutenant of the *Dolphin*, was given the command of the *Tamar*. Furthermore, he changed his plan. Instead of making for California, and looking for Davis Land on the way, he altered his course in 26° S. to N.W., in order to catch a trade wind and stretch across to the area where the Solomons were reported to lie. In doing so he was following almost the same track as Roggeveen. Like him he skirted the Tuamotu Archipelago and could not help falling in with some of its thousand islands. The first he called the Island of Disappointment, because no bottom could be found there, though he sounded with 140 fathom of line. However, 67 leagues to the westward he found what he called King George's Island, where some refreshment was to be had. It was all very well taking possession, but one of the first objects his men found was a broken Dutch rudder, perhaps from Roggeveen's *African Galley* which ran on a reef hereabouts. Prince of Wales and Duke of York's islands soon showed up, and so numerous were the atolls that he would soon have run through the names of the Royal Family had he not emerged from the archipelago. It is typical of the limitations of geographical knowledge that he at first mistook these for the Solomons, for it was here, half-way across the Pacific, that they were marked by the French in charts such as the *Neptune Français*.

As his water was running low and sickness was increasing he decided, in 8° S., to haul away to the northward in order to shape a course for the well known Marianas, Anson's luscious description of Tinian becoming daily more desirable in his eyes. In doing so his route begins to diverge from the general direction of the later Dutch voyagers which he had hitherto been following. He was able to add one small island to his small store of genuine discovery when he sighted what he called Byron Island, probably Onotoa or Nukunau in the south-east of the Gilbert group. It was inhabited by friendly copper-coloured

natives from whom coconuts were obtained and proved an
astonishingly effective cure for scurvy: those whose limbs were
as black as ink, and who could not move without excruciating
pain, were soon so far recovered that they could go aloft. But
as they continued northward, crossing the line in intense heat
the disease began to increase once more. None of the cases
proved fatal, but it was with immense relief that early in July
four months and twenty days from the Straits, the *Dolphin*
anchored in the same bay at Tinian as the *Centurion* had done
twenty-three years earlier.

Byron's men looked forward eagerly to tasting the delight
of the island. Water, fruit, and the invaluable coconut were
abundant, but their predecessor's account of orchards and lawns
and milk-white cattle appeared to be in the nature of a mirage
"I am indeed of the opinion," says Byron, "that this is one of
the most unhealthy spots in the world." The heat was worse
than anything he had experienced in Africa; the undergrowth
was so thick they could not catch the cattle; the place swarmed
with scorpions and ants; whenever those on shore opened their
mouths, flies and mosquitoes darted down their throats. Nine
weeks they stayed there, until nearly all the sick (including
Byron himself) were restored to health, in spite of the climate

Since he was now convinced that his work in the South Seas
was done, Byron made all speed for Batavia, in order to take
advantage of the monsoon. Just before he got there he spoke
with a snow belonging to the East India Company, the captain
of which gave him a sheep, a dozen fowls and a turtle; "this
was a most acceptable present, for we had nothing to eat but
the ship's provisions, which were become very bad. Our beef
and pork stunk intolerably, and our bread was rotten and full
of worms."

At Batavia, a "cockswain, a very ragged, dirty fellow,"
boarded the ship on behalf of the naval authorities. Pulling out
ink and paper, he proceeded to ask impertinent questions about
Byron's route. This was not the way to speak to a British officer
after the naval triumphs of the last war. "As I was impatient
to save him the trouble," remarks the Commodore, "he was

esired immediately to walk over the ship's side, and put off his oat, with which he was graciously pleased to comply."

An official visit to the Governor went off better, and Byron's fficers were comfortably lodged in the single palatial hotel the lace boasted. But, making the climate his excuse, he embarked again without delay. Three men died of a "putrid ever" in the Straits of Sunda—exactly half the total casualties f the whole voyage. It did not deter the rest from celebrating Christmas Day with such zeal that an officer complains "our eople were in high spirits, and not a little troublesome." One f them, a gunner, fell asleep afterwards with a pipe in his nouth and tumbled overboard, never to be seen again. On the vhole, however, Byron was justified in boasting on his return hat more men would have died had they stayed at home.

The rest of the voyage was made without incident, save that he *Tamar's* rudder was damaged and she had to be sent to the Vest Indies for repairs. After nine weeks' passage from the ape the *Dolphin* returned home on May 9, 1766. She had one round the world in 22 months, the fastest voyage yet ecorded, but also, it must be confessed, one of the most fruitless. xcept for the experience it gave to future explorers like arteret, little had been done of any value. Byron never had he patience or the curiosity of the true explorer. Having been old to survey the Falklands, all he did was to sail round the orth coast; having been told to visit New Albion, he took the hortest way home instead. With his reputation for bad luck, nd with the memory of the last English circumnavigation fresh i his mind, he congratulated himself on carrying out such a ifficult task with such a remarkable absence of casualties or icident.

Certainly the most important result was the staking out of he British claim to the Falklands. The anchor of the *Dolphin* ad hardly rattled out before the emissaries of the French and panish embassies were on the spot to bribe the crews into elling them something. They got little for their efforts. Agog r news, the Spanish Ambassador called on Lord Egmont, "the hief of the Admiralty," only to be told that the *Dolphin* had gone in search of survivors from the *Wager*. "There is a mystery in it," he wrote to Madrid, "because all the logs have been impounded." He knew that a frigate and two smaller ships had sailed on another mysterious errand the previous October, but he could not discover their names or their destination. (Actually they were the *Jason* frigate, *Carcass* sloop and *Experiment* storeship, which sailed on the return of the *Florida* in 1765 to lay the foundation of a settlement at Egmont on Byron's advice.) A month later the Ambassador was still fishing for information in a conversation with the Duke of Richmond. His Grace "replied in a bantering tone that they had been looking for giants."

"We could have saved them the trouble," replied His Excellency.

"Is the whole world Spain's?" inquired the Duke, somewhat nettled.

"I replied that, as to that portion, Yes."

Officers and crew being sworn to secrecy, the two Ambassadors could only work themselves into a frenzy of agitation about the destination of these expeditions: the Gallapagos of Peru? a North-West Passage? Juan Fernandez? the Falklands? It would be well, they warned their governments, to send out ships to see what was happening. But already, on the remote shores of the Falklands, matters were moving to a climax.

The paths of Byron and Bougainville first crossed when the *Dolphin* sighted the *Aigle* in the Straits of Magellan in February 1765. Though the two men never actually met, their subsequent careers are strangely parallel. Six months after Byron's return Bougainville, as we shall see, set out round the world by much the same route, though with greater good fortune. Both rose to the rank of admiral in their respective navies. Both were on the American station in the War of Independence. Their fleets met at the battle of Grenada in 1779, where Byron was in command of the British and Bougainville was one of his opponent's senior officers. Neither side acquitted itself well, Byron attacking in an impetuous manner and only escaping defeat by the incapacity of his opponent. This was Byron's last command, but Bougainville lived to run away at the battle of the Saints three years later. Both numbered poets among their descendants who made use of the exploits of their ancestors in their works: the shipwreck in *Don Juan* and *La Bouteille à la Mer* by Alfred de Vigny.

Bougainville was personally the more successful of the two. He forestalled Byron in the Falklands and found Tahiti, which the latter missed, and in spite of the Revolution he lived to an honoured old age. But when Byron died in 1786, he died, says an obituary notice, "with the universal and justly acquired reputation of a brave and excellent officer, but, of a man, extremely unfortunate." Foul Weather Jack was unfortunate not only in the weather, which on two occasions nearly terminated his career—the wreck of the *Wager* at the age of 17; and at the age of 55, when the fleet he commanded was almost totally dismasted in one of the most catastrophic Atlantic gales in naval history. He was also unfortunate in his family. While the *Dolphin* was in the South Seas his drunken father, "the wicked Lord Byron," killed a man after a club dinner. In a state trial he was convicted of manslaughter and only escaped punishment by virtue of his rank. He retired to Newstead Abbey a marked man, hated by his tenants, his wife and his children. Admiral John's eldest son, Mad Jack, was the handsome profligate who became the father of the poet. In four generations of Byrons, Admiral John was the only one who escaped the taint of insanity. And even he was of all men accounted the most unfortunate.

IX

THE *DOLPHIN* AND THE *SWALLOW*

IN the list of famous ships which have sailed across the widest ocean in the world—*Victoria, Golden Hind, Centurion, Adventure, Endeavour*—the *Dolphin* deserves to be remembered. In the space of four years, with the briefest interval to refit, she sailed twice round the world on two of the happiest voyages ever recorded. On her first voyage, in spite of a diversion to the Falklands, she took 688 days. On her second, in spite of an exceptionally slow passage of the Straits, she took only 637 days. The casualty list of both voyages numbered under a dozen. One would have thought her record a sufficiently good advertisement for copper bottoms, but not for more than ten years to come was the whole fleet so equipped.

Byron returned at the beginning of May 1766. Next month the *Dolphin* was recommissioned for another voyage to the Pacific, this time under the command of Captain Samuel Wallis, a phlegmatic individual who was ill for most of the voyage. His narrative, written in the polished impersonal style of the day, shows neither the observant eye of a Dampier, nor the colourful turn of phrase of an Elizabethan. His first lieutenant was Cummings, late captain of the *Tamar*, and his second lieutenant was Tobias Furneaux, later to command the *Adventure* under Cook. With him sailed Philip Carteret, Byron's Number One, in command of the *Swallow* sloop.

When it was hinted to Carteret that he was to take this thirty-year-old vessel in company with the *Dolphin*, whose sailing qualities he knew well, he could not believe it. He was sure that when his sealed orders were opened at sea he would find that he was to replace the *Jason* at the Falklands, for she was another coppered frigate of the same class as the *Dolphin*. Furthermore, Wallis' ship was exceptionally well equipped; even the captain's cabin was stuffed with stores: three thousand weight of portable soup, a bale of cork life-jackets, rolls of "fear-nought" cloth, and "an extraordinary quantity of medicine." Apart from being an exceptionally slow sailer (if ever a ship was mis-named she was the *Swallow*), with sheathing that was totally inadequate for a long voyage, not even a forge for repairs or a skiff for emergencies were provided. When her captain complained about the inadequacy of her equipment he was told that the *Dolphin* would provide. It did not occur to the inept administration of the day that two such incompatible ships were bound to get separated.

Carteret accepted his destiny with a fine equanimity—"I determined at all events to perform my duty in the best manner I was able." The crew, of course, sailed in happy ignorance of their fate; but once at sea rumours began to fly about, and Carteret was not surprised when nine of his best men jumped overboard at Madeira and swam, stark naked, to the shore. When they were brought back on board again, still without a stitch of clothing on them, Carteret demanded to know the reason for this attempt at desertion. They explained that they never meant to desert the ship; they only wanted to get a skinful of liquor before it was too late. With uncommon good sense the captain accepted this excuse, and for the rest of her long and hazardous voyage he never had the slightest difficulty with his men.

The news that the *Dolphin* was fitting out at Deptford soon reached the interested embassies in London. On July 25, 1766, a dockyard spy reported that she was destined for the Falklands, with other ships as storeships. All of which was pure invention. True, the *Prince Frederick* storeship was to sail to the Straits with Wallis, where she was to be detached to revictual the settlement at Port Egmont. But a letter from Their Lordships, dated August 16, shows that the destination of the *Dolphin* and the *Swallow* was far otherwise. "In case you shall meet with any Officer whose Seniority may render it proper for you to shew the Orders you are under, you are to carefully avoid letting him see the said Secret Orders, and to shew him only the said first mentioned Order directing you to proceed to the Leeward Islands."

The main objective was really *Terra Australis Incognita* The relevant passages in the Secret Orders, which have no hitherto been printed, are as follows:

> You are to proceed with the *Dolphin* and the *Swallou* round Cape Horn, or through the Straights of Magellan, a you shall find most convenient, and stretch to the Westward about One Hundred or One Hundred and Twenty Degrees o Longitude from Cape Horn, losing as little Southing as pos sible, in search of the Lands or Islands supposed to lie in tha part of the Southern Hemisphere which is before mentione (i.e. between Cape Horn and New Zealand), unless you sha discover such Lands or Islands in a shorter run, or shall hav been farther to the Northward than you might reasonabl have expected. . . .

> But if contrary to expectation you shall not have dis covered the Land or Islands supposed to lye in the Southern Hemisphere as before mentioned, in stretching to the West ward as before directed, you are then either to return t England round Cape Horn or to stand to the North West unti you get into the Latitude of 20° South in search of the Land or Islands that have not hitherto been discovered, and upon your arrival in that Latitude if you find the condition of the ship and sloop, and the State of their Provisions and the Health of their men will admit of your proceeding any farthe upon Discoveries of the like nature, you are at liberty to d so, taking care to reserve a sufficient quantity of Provision to enable you to proceed to China or some of the European Settlements in the East Indies, which you are in that case to do, in order to give your Men such Refreshment as they may stand in need of, and to put the ship and sloop into condition to return to England round the Cape of Good Hope and transmit to our Secretary for our information an Accoun of your arrival and proceedings.

On August 22, 1766, the two ships weighed and made sai down river. Before Christmas they were off the coast of Pata gonia, *Terra Gigantium* according to Byron. But Wallis, who measured the natives without their shoes on, found the tallest was 6 feet 7 inches and the majority about 6 feet. The crew, of course, would not willingly allow such a story to die. The ship's carpenter wrote home a letter which found its way into print, telling his brother that he had been "at the land of giants, of whom the biggest are 8 feet in height, but their ordinary stature is $7\frac{1}{2}$ feet."

On December 17 they entered the Straits, diverting the storeship with her decks loaded with saplings, their roots wrapped in earth, to the treeless Falklands. As Carteret was the most experienced officer, he was told to lead the *Dolphin* through the Straits. Continuous contrary winds delayed them to such an extent that theirs was the longest passage on record: 82 days from Port Famine to Cape Pillar, four months in the Straits as a whole. Seamen were allowed to explore the desolate shores, but found the habits of the Fuegians so disgusting that they "stunk like foxes." To Wallis' civilised eye the western reaches "had the appearance more of a chaos than of Nature. . . . As this seems to be the most dreary and inhospitable country in the world, so the people seem to be the lowest and most deplorable of all human beings."

On more than one occasion Carteret begged to be allowed to take the *Swallow* home; alternatively, in view of his experience in the South Seas, to come aboard the *Dolphin* and send his own ship home under the command of her first lieutenant. It was obvious to him that she could never cross the Pacific: already she was leaking badly and her rudder was damaged. But Wallis refused to take the responsibility of such a decision. Perhaps he hoped that circumstances would compel Carteret to turn back, as so many had done before. Indeed, when they neared the exit and an easterly breeze sprang up, the *Dolphin* shot past her consort and was soon lost to sight. Wallis' excuse for not shortening sail to wait for the *Swallow* was that the current was sweeping him back into the Straits. If, indeed, he did deliberately desert her, he was certainly mistaken in his estimation of Carteret's sense of duty. The captain of the *Swallow* was not

made of the same stuff as those renegades who parted company
with Drake and Anson hereabouts on much flimsier excuses.

The Humboldt current prevented Wallis from carrying out
his instructions to sail due west after issuing from the Straits.
As others before him, he was swept north, though he managed
to keep well to the west of Juan Fernandez.   In spite of every
precaution—a pint of pickled cabbage a day, wine instead of
spirits, hammocks aired and decks washed with vinegar, portable
soup, "sweet wort and salop"—scurvy began to affect the crew.
The disease never became serious, but they were glad enough to
sight their first Pacific islands in the Tuamotu Archipelago.   He
named them after members of the Royal Family—Queen
Charlotte, Gloucester, Cumberland, Osnabrugh (the Duke of
York had become bishop of this see at the age of seven months).
After setting up the flag, he made the pleasant gesture of leaving
a collection of hatchets, nails, glass bottles and coins "as presents
to the natives, and an atonement for the disturbances we had
given them."

The morning of June 19, 1767, dawned misty.   When the
fog lifted, those on board the *Dolphin* found themselves surrounded by hundreds of canoes of all types, and as visibility
increased an entrancing prospect opened before them: the
wooded peaks, with the morning mist still wreathing them, of
the island of Tahiti.   Wallis gave this, the largest island of the
Society group, the inappropriate name of King George III
Island, but even his dull soul was touched by its beauty.

"A fine, stout, lively boy" was the first up the ship's side,
followed by a swarm of other equally magnificent physical
specimens.   They were all over the ship in a moment, stealing
things right and left.   One jumped overboard with an officer's
lace hat.   Another, butted in the stern by the ship's goat, took
a flying leap in terror of the strange animal.   "All the rest,
upon seeing what had happened, followed his example with the
utmost precipitation."

The *Dolphin* sailed leisurely along the southern coast in
search of an anchorage, but the canoes seemed determined to
attack.   Showers of stones rattled down on the deck, and the

flotilla had to be dispersed by firing a gun. Both Wallis and his first lieutenant were ill at the time, so Furneaux had to lead the watering party to take possession and hoist the flag. They were welcomed by a crowd of women, who proceeded to dance in such a remarkably indecent manner, with "wanton gestures, the meaning of which could not possibly be mistaken," that even sailors accustomed to orgies in port were properly shocked. When their enticing postures appeared to have no effect on these phlegmatic strangers, the women pelted them with bananas and apples, "shewing every mark of derision and contempt." In this garden of Eden, it was certainly Eve who tempted Adam.

The throb of drums at night gave warning of another attack. At dawn Wallis saw through his telescope that the flag had been pulled down. Everywhere he could discern groups of natives creeping into ambushes. Divisions of canoes swept into the bay, some with a new form of diversionary warfare on board: "ladies practising their allurements." Meanwhile an assemblage of children and civilians collected at a point of vantage to see the fun. Operations appeared to be conducted from a large double canoe, a sort of gondola with a canopy at the stern, in which sat persons of obvious importance, entertained by a band of flautists. When about 300 canoes, manned by at least 2000 men, had collected Wallis gave the order to fire with small shot. The canoes dispersed, and then collected again. So the "great guns" were directed at the chief's canoe and split it in two. The report of the guns echoed round the bay. Women ran screaming inland, and the canoes paddled rapidly round the cape.

It is surprising that amicable relations were restored so soon after this encounter. But watering parties met with gifts and every sign of welcome. Tents for the sick were erected on shore, and the surgeon went duck shooting. When, to the amazement of the spectators (and not least to the surgeon himself) three duck fell to one barrel, the superiority of the white man was definitely established. The mere sight of a musket was enough to deter the most mischievous islander. For the rest of their stay the visitors fared sumptuously every day.

After food and water, women, of course, were the principal

attraction, those fatal beauties whose daughters proved the undoing of the *Bounty* twenty years later. Indeed, had there been a Fletcher Christian in the *Dolphin*, the same fate might have overtaken her. Chastity, Wallis remarks dryly, does not appear to be a virtue among them. A nail was enough to purchase their favours. In a few days every scrap of iron in the ship had vanished, and the men were even pulling the nails out of the planks. "To preserve the ship from being pulled to pieces, I ordered that no man, except the wooders and waterers, with their guard, should be permitted to go on shore." Defaulters had to be flogged and discipline was visibly weakening. Midshipman Ibbot gives some description of the attractions of those dusky beauties in his unpublished diary, but nothing like so lively an account as that provided by the French visitors next year, or by Surgeon Hamilton in his journal of the voyage of H.M.S. *Pandora* in search of those of the *Bounty* who had succumbed to them. Ibbot was intrigued by the tattooing of the belly and the thighs—"having their Backsides Black'd." Though the common sort of girl sold herself for a nail, "Yet I must say yt, the Girls wh. were of the whiter sort would admit of any freedom except the last, which they would not, every one having a Man or Husband."

The land of sunshine and syphilis. . . . Who was responsible for the introduction of the latter? Bougainville, arriving eight months later, accuses Wallis. Wallis returns the charge, exculpating himself on the evidence of his surgeon's log, which proved his crew to have been entirely free for the six months preceding their arrival and for six months after. The Tahitian whom Bougainville took on board was riddled with it and appeared to think nothing of it; perhaps, it has been suggested, he mistook the symptoms of yaws, a common disease in the Pacific. The evidence is so contradictory that we can never know the truth.

"On Saturday, July 11, the gunner came on board with a tall woman, who seemed about five and fourty years of age, of a pleasing countenance and majestic deportment." This was O Berea the queen, "the stoutest woaman I ever saw," says

Midshipman Ibbot. She had been away in the interior when they arrived. In spite of the Captain's indisposition she insisted on his visiting her on shore, carrying him over streams and rough places as if he had been a child. When they reached her palatial hut, four girls were ordered to massage him and his lieutenant. This delightful treatment was interrupted by screams from without. The surgeon, finding the day warm, had removed his wig. Nothing so shocking had ever been seen on the island before. Meanwhile Furneaux and the mate were conducted on expeditions inland, as a result of which they confirmed the impression that this was a paradise indeed. Everywhere fruit, flowers and water abounded. There were no signs of beasts of prey or reptiles. Life would have passed as happily as in the Golden Age if it were not for the ubiquitous ants.

It was time to be moving on, after tasting the delights of the island for a month. When O Berea was told of their intention, she burst into a flood of tears. We will be back in fifty days, promised Wallis; but it was Bougainville, not Wallis, who next appeared, and O Berea was not there to welcome him; and when Cook met her a year later she had fallen from her high estate.

As they ran westward through the fringe of the Society group they discovered so many islands that Wallis, having exhausted the Royal Family, had to fall back on distinguished admirals. The names of Keppel, Boscawen, Saunders, as well as the Scillies, are here commemorated. It was at this point that the Captain made up his mind to continue round the world and not return the way he had come, as he seems to have intended at first. Tinian was his next objective, which he reached by sailing to the west of the Marshall and Gilbert groups, not to the east as Byron had done. Wallis Island (Uvea, north of the Tonga group) marks his track. Tinian, of course, was a disappointment after Tahiti, but most of the sick (though not he himself) recovered there. When the ship reached Batavia at the end of November there was only one sick man on board. It was as happy a crossing of the Pacific as has ever been made —in striking contrast to the experience of the *Swallow*, as will be seen.

In spite of the curiosity of the Dutch, Wallis strictly obeyed the secrecy imposed upon him. His crew was forbidden to land on the excuse of the danger of getting drunk on arrack. The Captain's restraint had a pathetic consequence. Near the harbour he found the derelict *Falmouth* man-of-war, damaged after the attack on Manila during the late war. Her crew had never been able to get a passage home. They had no money, and the Dutch refused to allow them to spend a single night on shore. In that rotten hulk the poor wretches lived for eight years, robbed by the Malays, insulted by the Dutch, dying of disease, and, most intolerable of all, neglected by their own government. Wallis promised to do his best for them on his return, but nothing came of it.

As Byron found before him, and Carteret after him, the Dutch at the Cape were far more hospitable than the jealous merchants of the East. Having watered there, the *Dolphin* sped home. She anchored in the Downs on May 20, 1768, after beating Byron's record for a circumnavigation, and that in spite of the fact that Wallis always lay to at night in order not to miss making fresh discoveries.

The news of the discovery of Tahiti, the most important yet made by an Englishman in the Pacific, was soon out. *Lloyd's Evening Post* of May 23 announced the discovery of "a large, fertile and extremely populous island in the South Seas." Believers in *Terra Australis* were much encouraged, and the Spanish Ambassador expressed his usual misgivings. Wallis, he reported, had seen the King; it was probable that a colony had been founded in seas "where the ships of that nation used formerly not to go"; he had bribed a seaman to get news, but the logs were impounded; meanwhile it was up to his government to argue that what Wallis had found had previously been discovered by Quiros.

We left Captain Carteret watching the topsails of the *Dolphin* disappearing over the western horizon. Studding sails too; it looked as if Wallis did not intend to wait for him. No rendezvous had been agreed upon, and it was vain to think of atching up with the *Dolphin*. The unlucky *Swallow* was too heavy a sailer to take advantage of the momentary easterly breeze which carried the *Dolphin* out of the Straits. When the wind shifted to the west again, she had the greatest difficulty in weathering Cape Pillar. As a wise captain, Carteret took the crew into his confidence, and appealed to their loyalty to work the ship home: "I had the satisfaction to see no marks of despondency among my people, whom I encouraged, by telling them, that although the *Dolphin* was the best ship, I did not doubt but that I should find more than equivalent advantages in their courage, ability, and good conduct."

He soon encountered far worse weather than he ever experienced under Foul Weather Jack. "A prodigious swell from the north west" sent seas crashing over the fo'c'sle, sweeping along the decks. Constantly the bowsprit buried itself in mountainous rollers, so that they shipped it green at every impact, but they managed to break the force of the water by erecting bulkheads along the decks. For days they lay under bare poles, not daring to show any canvas, "and the water at times was torn up, and whirled around in the air, much higher than the masts heads." Surely she must founder, but "with all her defects, we must acknowledge that she was indeed a good sea boat."

Juan Fernandez they found to be fortified, probably in consequence of suggestions on the part of the Spanish Ambassador in London. So they turned away to the neighbouring Masafuera. Here surf forbade the approach of a boat. Their need for water was desperate, so the captain called for volunteers from among his Madeira swimmers, who stripped and jumped into the boiling sea with casks lashed to their shoulders. The surf increasing, they were unable to swim back to the ship and had to spend the night on shore, naked and shivering, without fire or food. They were taken off the next morning none the worse for their privations.

As soon as weather permitted they continued on a north-westerly course in search of Davis Land. Just as Roggeveen had discovered Easter Island on such a search, so Carteret discovered

K

the rocky islet of Pitcairn, named after the junior officer wh
sighted it.   It achieved notoriety thirty years later when th
Bounty mutineers settled there with their Tahitian mistresses
Turning west, so that his route took him well to the south o
Tahiti, Carteret found various atolls which, like Wallis, he named
after members of the Royal Family; but they afforded him n
refreshment, and he was forced to rely on an awning stretched
across the deck for his supply of water.   Rain water, mixed with
spirits of vitriol, was an excellent anti-scorbutic, affirmed the
surgeon.

He was wrong.   Scurvy casualties soon reached dangerou
proportions among the exhausted crew.   Carteret was compelled
to turn north in search of a trade wind.   His route was, in fact
almost the same as Schouten's, and somewhat to the south o
that followed by the *Dolphin*.   He expected daily to find the
Solomons, but, like Byron, he could find no trace of them in the
position given by French cartographers.   They were now in
mid-ocean, with a quarter of the crew down with scurvy, the
captain and the first lieutenant ill, the ship refusing to answer
the helm, and leaks below the water-line increasing daily.   In
this desperate situation they had the good fortune, on August 12,
1767, to find what Carteret rightly guessed to be the Santa Cruz
islands.   He renamed them Queen Charlotte's Islands, and the
best anchorage, New Guernsey, after his native land.   The
names have not survived, but those of Howe and Swallow are
still to be found on the map.   As in the days of Quiros and
Mendaña, the natives proved extremely hostile, advancing
resolutely with bows and arrows in spite of the proffered beads
and ribbons.   The Master returned from the first boat party
with three arrows sticking into him.   Like the Spaniards, they
had to water by force, dispelling the lurking savages with
musketry.   Instead of enjoying the delights of the island, as
their friends were doing at Tahiti over 2000 miles to the east
of them, the crew of the *Swallow* had the mortification of sailing
along palmy shores, seeing the bananas, the coconuts, the hogs
and poultry on shore, without being able to get at them.   Like
Quiros, Carteret seems to have been convinced that land lay to

risen to 24, apart from those dangerously ill. Had he not taken on some of the *Falmouth's* men he would never have worked the ship home.

On February 19, 1769, more than a year after reaching Macassar, the *Swallow* was overhauled in mid-Atlantic by a strange sail. A boat pulled across and a French officer came on board. After saluting Carteret by name, he said that his ship was a French East Indiaman from Mauritius, commanded by a M. de Bougainville. Carteret could not understand how the Frenchman was so well acquainted with him, until he was told that a bottle containing particulars about the ship, which had been left at Ascension, had been picked up by him a few days previously. Even then the Frenchman's curiosity seemed excessive. "He began to propose his questions in direct terms, and desired to know on which side of the Equator I had crossed the South Seas. As I did not think proper to answer this question, and wished to prevent others of the same kind, I rose up somewhat abruptly, and, I believe, with some marks of displeasure." Instead of information, the visitor was given a Santa Cruz arrow as a present for his captain.

Meanwhile the boat's crew had got into conversation, from which it appeared that the ship was not an East Indiaman at all, but the frigate *La Boudeuse*, returning, like themselves, from a voyage round the world. Not till much later did Carteret learn how closely Bougainville had followed him across the Pacific, and he expressed his extreme annoyance at the underhand way in which his rival had contrived to get information out of him.

Soon after, "though the French ship was foul after a long voyage, and we had just been cleaned, she shot by us as if we had been at anchor, notwithstanding we had a fine fresh gale and all our sails set." Bougainville was equally impressed by the state of the *Swallow*. "His ship was very small, went very ill, and when we took leave of him, he remained as it were at anchor. How much he must have suffered in so bad a vessel may well be conceived."

The little *Swallow* reached Spithead on March 20, 1769.

Carteret's determination in sailing her round the world on his own initiative, when he could so easily have turned back, does him the highest credit. His pluck and well-deserved good fortune in making such valuable rediscoveries puts his voyage on a level with the heroic enterprises of the sixteenth century, than which there can be no higher praise.

X

BOUGAINVILLE AND THE NOBLE SAVAGE

THE figure of Count Louis Antoine de Bougainville has already crossed these pages. In his contacts with the British, in Canada, in the South Seas, in the West Indies, he was indeed invariably unfortunate; but in his own country he won great fame as soldier, sailor and author. Today his memory is recalled, if at all, by the ostentatious *Bougainvillea* creeper, which the botanist he took with him on his voyage round the world discovered at Tahiti; and by the island in the Solomons which bears his name. In his own day his fame rested chiefly on his achievements as the first French circumnavigator. The success of his narrative was enormous, and those pages in which he describes his visit to Tahiti reached a much wider public than that normally interested in geographical matters. In consequence, they exerted considerable influence on the evolution of social and political ideals, particularly those connected with the state of nature and the noble savage.

Evidently Bougainville was a man of great charm and versatility. His plump figure, his unflagging enthusiasm for food, women, mathematics and adventure makes him an endearing figure. No book of travels in English, apart from Dampier and the Elizabethans, can equal his penetrating and lucid account. Contemporary English narratives are dull and provincial compared with the elegance of this, for its author represents the main stream of European culture at a time when French influence was predominant. He was, indeed, very much more than a sailor, which is more than can be said of his English rivals. At twenty-two he published a treatise on the integral calculus; at thirty he was aide-de-camp to Montcalm and assisted at the defence of Quebec; soon after, he helped to negotiate the peace treaty. He was a Fellow of the Royal Society and a Member of the Institute. Not content with a reputation as a soldier, diplomatist and scientist, his far-ranging enthusiasm led him to embrace the career of a seaman.

If men of his stamp had received the support they deserved, the story of French colonial enterprise in the eighteenth century would have been far different. Moreover, if the Court was apathetic, the opposition was definitely hostile. "France can be happy without Quebec," wrote Voltaire after the struggle: if there was anything on which the Encyclopaedists were agreed it was the vanity of colonies. They attacked the imperialists with every weapon in their formidable armoury, though that did not stop them from playing at savages at home in order to castigate the sins of society. To a man like Diderot, Bougainville was merely a "leader of brigands," fouling the innocence of the South Seas. Yet today Tahiti is part of the French empire, and the nonsense that was talked about the noble savage is forgotten, except perhaps among the followers of D. H. Lawrence. Of course, as far as Bougainville and his like were the precursors of that horde of expropriators which were soon to descend like a blight upon the Pacific, the attack is justifiable. But was the state of nature so very enviable? The Marquesas may have been ruined and depopulated by the white man, but what about Fiji and Samoa?

After the loss of Canada Bougainville was the first to appreciate the importance of the South Seas as an alternative. To him, as to Anson, the key lay in the Falklands. Well aware of British pretensions in those parts, he determined to forestall them. In 1763 he fitted out at his own expense two ships at St. Malo to transport some families of Acadian loyalists, now dispossessed by the British. On the first voyage Port Louis in Berkeley Sound was founded, and when he returned next year he found his colony in a flourishing condition. It was on this visit, while engaged in bringing timber from the Straits of Magellan, that he encountered Byron's *Dolphin*. Before he could visit his colony a third time Captain Macbride of the *Jason* (sent out in pursuance of Byron's advice) had discovered his settlement. He brusquely demanded of the French governor, on what authority he had erected a settlement on British territory. The latter, having been there for three years, showed some surprise; whereupon Macbride changed his tone and explained that he had only come to survey the islands.

Meanwhile the barren outpost had been drawn into the web of international politics. The official French policy adopted by the Duc de Choiseul involved the collapse of Bougainville's whole scheme. Nursing schemes of revenge against the British, and realising the insecurity of his position at the Court of Versailles, de Choiseul was prepared to go to any lengths to prove that his talents were indispensable to France. The first step was to win Spain to his side. The next, to use her as a stalking horse to provoke a quarrel with Britain. Bougainville's colony was the obvious bait. For some time Spain had been mildly protesting at the presence of the French off the American coast. The easiest way to win her favour was to send Bougainville to Madrid to sell his settlement.

The unfortunate founder discovered that his colony was worth exactly 618,108 *livres*, 13 *sols* and 11 *deniers* in the international market. Having completed the sale, Choiseul waited for the British to commit the inevitable act of aggression. In August 1766 Wallis sailed, presumably for the Falklands, according to information received from the French embassy. In November Bougainville sailed to hand over the colony in person to the Spanish authorities in South America. Having done so, he was instructed to continue across the Pacific, evidently with the aim of claiming any new discovery as a substitute for the lost islands. Wallis, however, never went near the Falklands, thereby gaining a big start on the French expedition, with the result that he succeeded in making discoveries which would otherwise have been Bougainville's.

The two French ships were *La Boudeuse*, a 26-gun frigate with a crew of 200, and *L'Étoile*, which had previously taken Bougainville to the Falklands. He preferred the latter as a more seaworthy vessel as she carried less weight of guns, and he originally intended to sail round the world in her, sending back any of his colonists who wished to be repatriated in the *Boudeuse*. But *L'Étoile* was so badly damaged by an

Atlantic gale that he decided for safety's sake to take both ships with him.

The first official French expedition to the Pacific was of a new kind—a scientific expedition of the type familiar to us from the examples of Cook and Darwin and Shackleton. Two notable scientists were on board: the botanist Commerson and the astronomer Verron (or Véron). Philibert Commerson did not relish the prospect of such a voyage. Of an eccentric and unsociable temperament, he disliked everything about the sea and those who sailed on it. About Verron we know little beyond the fact that his mission was to discover a better method of finding longitude at sea. He brought on board an instrument called a megameter, but Bougainville admits that Hadley's quadrant was a far more efficient means of discovering time by means of "lunars." Since this meant measuring "the distances of the moon from the sun, or from the stars in the zodiac" and then calculating with lunar tables, the result was far from satisfactory. Unknown to the French, Harrison had just perfected the true solution with his marine time-piece; nor did the new English *Nautical Almanac* (composed by the Astronomer Royal, a firm believer in lunar method, and hence the chief stumbling-block in Harrison's path) appear until after they had sailed.

There were also several distinguished volunteers on board. The Prince of Nassau, for example, a soldier of fortune aged 21, who had already sold his sword to most of the European powers. There was also Pierre Fesche, another young man of good family, an ardent Rousseauist of a highly inflammable temperament. Most of these gentlemen, together with Vivès the surgeon and St. Germain the ship's writer, left journals which have gradually come to light in recent years to corroborate Bougainville's official account and add something about what went on behind the commander's back.

Having handed over his colony to the Spanish authorities in South America, Bougainville reached the opening of the Straits of Magellan on December 2, 1767. Using old charts, Narborough's in particular, he made a safe passage through them in fifty-two days. Traces of the English were found wherever landings were made: knives and pieces of red cloth left by Byron, the initials of Wallis' men carved on trees. Objects dated 1766 and 1767 were found among the debris of a recent encampment. Bougainville could no longer have any doubt that he was following his rivals into the Pacific. Like them, he measured the Patagonians and found their height to be between 5 ft. 10 ins. and 6 ft. 2 ins. Nor did he have any more use for the "troublesome and disgusting" Fuegians. His observations on this race—their "insupportable stench" and "hideous women" —are interesting because the Rousseauists discreetly omit mentioning them. They focussed their attention on the noble creatures of Tahiti, whom they viewed through rose-coloured spectacles. But Bougainville is careful to point out that the Fuegians also lived "exactly in what may be called a state of nature." (Or, as Darwin put it, "I believe in this extreme part of the world man exists in a lower state of improvement than in any other.") From which Bougainville concluded that, after all, civilisation may be said to have conferred some benefits on the human race—a highly unpopular observation at the time.

Emerging from the Straits towards the end of January 1768, he disposed his two ships so as to cover as much of the ocean as possible without losing touch with each other. During the day *L'Étoile* was to sail on a parallel course to the southward, closing up astern of the *Boudeuse* when darkness fell. At first course was set for Juan Fernandez, but finding a trade wind in a higher latitude than he expected he put before it in the direction of the supposed Davis Land. Like Carteret, he soon concluded that it did not exist. Turning west, he first sighted land in the shape of numerous atolls forming the northern part of the Tuamotu Archipelago, which he identified with Roggeveen's Labyrinth and Quiros' Sagitaria.

The disciples of Quiros supposed these islands to be the outliers of the southern continent. On that subject the sceptical Bougainville makes a comment worthy of such a representative of the Age of Enlightenment. While agreeing that the existence of so many islands and "drowned lands" supported the theory, he adds, "Geography is a science of facts; in studying it, authors must by no means give way to any system, formed in their studies, unless they would run the risk of being subject to very great errors, which can be rectified only at the expense of navigators." No wonder that Dalrymple, who had just compiled a collection of voyages to prove the existence of a continent, disapproved of Bougainville.

On April 4, 1768, came the climax of the voyage: the sight of the northern shores of Tahiti. Unknown to the French, Wallis had sailed from his anchorage on the southern side exactly eight months previously.

From the sea the beauty of the island was indeed *saisissante*— the emerald of the coastal vegetation fading into the amethyst of the mountains inland. Their initiation to this new home of Venus, *La Nouvelle Cythère* as it came to be called, was entirely in character. From the scores of canoes that put out to greet them beautiful youths pointed with unequivocal gestures to the radiant *café-au-lait* coloured young women who accompanied them. "It was very difficult," says Bougainville benignly, "amidst such a sight, to keep at their work four hundred young French sailors, who had seen no women for six months. In spite of all our precautions, a young girl came on board, and placed herself upon the quarter-deck, near one of the hatchways, which was open in order to give air to those who were heaving the capstan below. The girl carelessly dropped a cloth which covered her, and appeared to the eyes of all beholders such as Venus showed herself to the Phrygian shepherd, having indeed the celestial form of that goddess. Both sailors and soldiers endeavoured to come to the hatchway; and the capstan was never hove with more alacrity than on this occasion." *Nous tombons en extase*, writes the impressionable Fesche; *une chaleur vive et douce s'empare de nos sens; nous brûlons. . . .*

The chief who met Bougainville as he stepped ashore was not O Berea, the queen of the south, the friend of Wallis and Cook, but a dignified old man named Ereti. He appeared to be in two minds as to how to receive his visitors, for he retired to his hut when they bowed before him. "His thoughtful and suspicious

air seemed to show that he feared the arrival of a new race of
men, who would trouble those happy days which he had spent
in peace." What an opening for the anti-imperialists!

However, the polished manners of the Frenchmen soon over-
came his natural hesitation. Nails and iron were asked for and
liberally distributed. (How was it, Bougainville asked himself,
that the word was pronounced in such a remarkably English
manner?). The strangers were asked how long they intended to
stay. Eighteen days, replied Bougainville. That was too long,
said Ereti; nine days will be quite enough. Bougainville shook
his head, nor would he agree to a request to spend the night on
board ship, for the sick had to be brought ashore. In point of
fact he only stayed eight days; but what a carnival week that
was!

As they returned to the boats "we were stopped by a fine-
looking islander who, lying under a tree, invited us to sit down
by him on the grass. We accepted his offer; he then leaned
towards us, and with a tender air, he slowly sung a song, without
doubt of Anacreontic kind, to the tune of a flute, which another
Indian blew with his nose: this was a charming scene, and
worthy of the pencil of a Boucher."

Another Garden of Eden, a veritable *champs élysées* they
called it. Commerson the Rousseauist went into raptures about
it: *cette isle me parut telle que je lui avois déjà appliqué le nom
d'Utopie ou de fortunée. . . . Et quelles femmes encore! Les rivals
des Georgiennes pour la beauté, et les sœurs des Graces sans voiles.
Là, ni la honte ni la pudeur n'exercent point leur tyrannie.* In
his eyes, gifts of knives and scissors were themselves crimes; as
for the thieving proclivities of the islanders, that was a mere
game. Bougainville, who lost a pistol while enjoying the hospitality of the chief's wives, could hardly be expected to see
things in that light.

All agree that Tahitian wives remained faithful to their
husbands on pain of death. But what was so delightful to these
Frenchmen was that jealousy seemed to be unknown. It was not
so much a question of obtaining the husband's permission, as of
refusing his solicitations. As for the unmarried, chastity was

definitely not regarded as a virtue. The young Prince of
Nassau, suffering from an *embarras des femmes*, was forced to
complain that, however pretty the girl, *les préjugées européens
exigent plus de mystère*.

The more they saw of the island the more unblemished did
its innocence appear to be. Even when four natives were accidentally shot by some soldiers, their compatriots begged the
commander to spare the lives of the culprits. But, in Bougainville's considered opinion, there was something wrong with this
paradise. The islanders' mode of existence was altogether too
easy. It made them beautiful and healthy, but it made them
lazy. Like children, they were the slaves of their passions: they
could not concentrate on anything for long. He learnt more of
the other side of the medal in conversation with Aotourou, the
islander he brought back with him to France. Aspects of life
which were not in evidence during a week's visit of untram-
melled happiness began to cast shadows over the bright picture
formed by first impressions: constant war with neighbouring
islands, infanticide, the killing of prisoners, syphilis, human
sacrifice. When Aotourou came across natives who did not
understand his language he petulantly ordered Bougainville to
exterminate them. So much for the noble savage. The
unwelcome conclusion that man is *not* born good forced itself
on his mind.

Aotourou was responsible for a very curious episode that
occurred soon after they left Tahiti. When the young man
came on board on their arrival he found himself the centre of
an inquisitive crowd of sailors. Amongst them was Commerson's valet named Baré. At the sight of the latter he immediately shouted the Tahitian word for "girl," and began making
what can only be called indelicate advances in the direction of
the valet, who fled, blushing furiously. Some weeks later Baré
appeared before Bougainville to confess what most of the crew
already suspected, that she was a woman. She told the captain
a hard-luck story about being an orphan reduced to a state of
destitution, which had compelled her to adopt her present
disguise. The truth was far otherwise. She was really Com-

merson's mistress—the unsociable Commerson who left a large sum of money to found a *Prix de Vertu*!

The first to guess the existence of a mystery was the surgeon Vivès, who could not understand why the seasick botanist should insist on his valet sharing his cabin. The hairless chin and retiring habits of M. de Commerson's valet soon led to rumours on the lower deck, rumours which Baré strove to dispel by excessively mannish behaviour. So it was not until she was mobbed by the women of Tahiti on her first landing there that these suspicions were taken seriously. "It must be owned," comments Bougainville, "that if the two ships had been wrecked on some desert isle, Baré's fate would have been a very singular one." She followed her master ashore when he was left behind at Mauritius, benefited by his will, and returned to die in France. Jeanne Baré has, therefore, the honour of being the first woman to sail round the world.

After leaving Tahiti Bougainville sighted any number of small islands. What he calls the Archipelago of Navigators must have been the Samoan group. Emerging from this, he discovered the lonely atoll of L'Enfant Perdu, still to be found by that name on some maps. Passing north of Fiji he reached the northern Cyclades, now the Anglo-French condominium of the New Hebrides. Just to the east of what he correctly identified as Quiros' Santo he named various islands—Isle d'Aurore, Isle de Lèpres, Isle de Pentecôte. Unfortunately, as others had found before him, the inhabitants were squat, ugly and hostile. Each island in turn refused him the refreshment he so anxiously demanded. As he sailed down their coasts "the negroes howled excessively in the woods, whither they had all retired, and where we could hear their drums beating." He was forced to continue west through the strait between Santo and Malekula which now bears his name.

At this point of the voyage the vital question arose as to whether this land of Quiros' was really a part of the continent, as its discoverer asserted. Was Santo connected with New Holland, as De Brosses suggested, or with New Guinea? It was certainly not joined to lands farther south. Only Dalrymple

could have told him that Torres had already proved that, and
had shown that a strait did really exist between New Guinea and
Australia.   Had Bougainville known the results of Torres'
voyage his own would have been far easier but far less
important.

To solve the problem he decided to continue west along the
fifteenth parallel, if necessary for a thousand miles.   What he
hoped to find was the eastern coast of Australia, and he got within
a hundred miles of doing so.   But on June 4 breaking seas dead
ahead of the *Boudeuse* forced him to turn sharply north.   The
obstacle which robbed him of the honour of discovering the
eastern coastline was that section of the Great Barrier Reef now
known as Bougainville Reef, a hundred miles east of Cooktown,
Queensland.   Like Cook, he very nearly lost his life there.
Though many on board were convinced that land lay to the
south-west, and he himself guessed that the reef was "nothing
less than the eastern coast of New Holland," it was essential
to turn north in order to save their ships and their
lives.

The situation on board was becoming desperate.   They had
had no chance to refresh themselves for two months.   Scurvy
was rife, though its incidence was checked by a liberal issue of
lemonade mixed with wine.   The distilling apparatus they
carried saved them from the extreme horrors of thirst, but of
food there was hardly any.   "I ate a rat yesterday with the
Prince of Nassau," writes the surgeon; "we found it excellent,
and wish there were more of them, provided no one else
wants to share them. . . . We had a stew for supper, made
from our leathern flasks, but it was not nearly so good as
the rat."

As they steered north through the Coral Sea a delicious smell
announced the vicinity of land.   It was the southern coast of
Papua.   But they were fearful of anchoring in uncharted
waters, and they could discern no break in the sweep of coast
slanting away to the south-east.   Bougainville thought it too
risky a business to steer west, though wind and current impelled
them in that direction, for it was very far from certain that New

Guinea and New Holland were separated. "Nothing, indeed, was more probable than the existence of such a passage," yet it was safer, in his view, to beat to windward to get out of the gulf and resume the run north to the safety of New Britain, with which he was familiar from Dampier's account. Cook, on the other hand, persisted in sailing west to escape from a similar predicament, and thereby rediscovered the Torres Strait.

But Bougainville found his own reward. After battling for fourteen critical days against wind and water to escape from the ring of breakers which threatened to embay them, they at last rounded the easterly cape of the Louisiade Archipelago and were able to resume their course northwards. "All the navigators who ever came into these parts always dreaded to fall to the southward of New Guinea, and of finding a gulf there corresponding to that of Carpentaria, which it would have proved difficult for them to clear. Consequently they have all in good time got into the latitude of New Britain (as Carteret had done the previous year, and as Schouten and Roggeveen had done earlier). They all followed the same track; we opened a new one, and paid dear for the honour of the first discovery."

Bougainville, in fact, was now sailing up the western shores of the Solomons, whereas Carteret had been sailing up the eastern coast. Both were making for the same haven, and both were ignorant of the true character of what they discovered on the way thither. The first land Bougainville sighted on his starboard bow was the island he named Choiseul. Sailing between it and the island which now bears his name, he passed through the Bougainville Strait, the pre-war boundary between the Australian and British mandates in the Solomons. He does not seem to have had the least idea of the size of his island. All he says is that "on July 3 in the morning we saw nothing but the new coast which is of a surprising height, and which lies N.W. by W."

On the next day a smaller island appeared, from which frizzly-haired natives of a remarkable blue-black pigmentation put off in canoes shouting, *Bouca, Bouca,* by which they appeared to mean coconuts. So the island was called Buka. Steering round the north of it (as Carteret had done), Bougainville reached New Britain two days later.

Such is the story of the re-discovery of the Solomons. But their identity had not yet been proved. The next year the French explorer Surville, on his ill-fated voyage eastward across the Pacific, visited the northern islands without recognising them for what they were; nor did Lieut. Shortland, R.N., when he visited the southern islands in 1788.[1] Thinking them a new discovery he named them New Georgia, which remains the name of one of the largest islands. Soon afterwards, in 1793, D'Entrecasteaux, in search of La Pérouse who had mysteriously disappeared hereabouts, sighted them once more. Neither he, nor Surville, nor La Pérouse, ever returned, but before his death he had achieved the secondary aim of his voyage: the identification of the Solomons. Their restoration to the map was really due to the brilliant hypothesis of two academic geographers: Philippe Buâche, "*premier géographe du roi*," and Captain Claret de Fleurieu, an important figure in French naval administration at that date. In a contribution to the Academy of Sciences in 1781 Buâche wrote, "I think I can with confidence assert that the Lands of the Arsacides (Surville's name for the inhospitable inhabitants of the central islands; he meant 'assassin') and Choiseul Bay (Bougainville's name) are parts of the archipelago discovered by Mendaña; and consequently that the Islands of Solomon are actually about 1850 Spanish leagues distant from the coast of Peru, and in the vicinity of New Guinea, as the early charts had indicated." The Ortelius atlas of 1589 (see frontispiece) shows them approximately in this position. But Robert Dudley's map of 1644 transferred them to the Marquesas, also discovered by Mendaña. In the next century Delisle followed him in this, Danville suppressed them altogether, and Dalrymple confused them with New Britain. By detecting these errors Buâche was able to restore the probable position of the islands to the spot where the earlier maps had shown them. Ten years later, in a study of the French voyages of 1768-9, published

---

[1] See page 167.

Plate V

WALLIS AT TAHITI

From Hawkesworth's *Voyages*, 1773

Plate VI

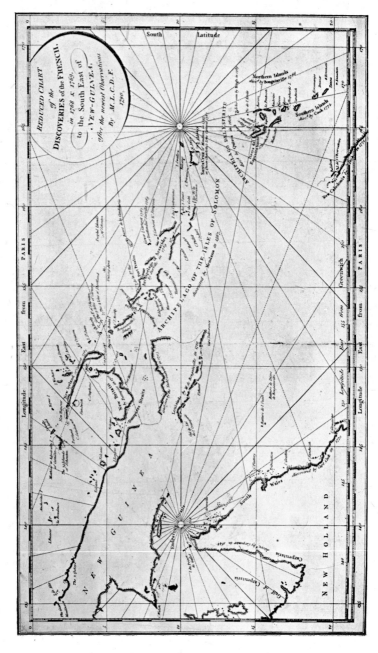

in 1790, Fleurieu presented the chart which is here reproduced opposite page 163. It shows all that was then known of the one area in the Pacific which Cook omitted to visit; but, as Fleurieu admits, the theory was far from proven and "all this part still offers a vast field to the researches of navigators." Fortunately he was able to prepare the instructions for D'Entrecasteaux, and the officers who returned from that voyage were able to confirm the accuracy of his charts which had been based on Buâche's hypothesis. Thus, after an interval of two hundred years, the Solomons were restored to their rightful place on the map; but the interior of the islands (as of New Guinea) remained largely unexplored at the outbreak of the present war. Even the eastern coasts of New Guinea were not charted until 1873, when Captain Moresby visited the area in H.M.S. *Basilisk*.

At Dampier's St. George's Bay, near the modern Wide Bay, Bougainville found the rest and refreshment he had sorely needed for the past three months. But he had not been there forty-eight hours when a sailor, searching the shore for shellfish, made the unwelcome discovery of a lead plate half buried in the sand. On it these letters could be traced:

- - - - HOR'D HERE
- - - - ICK MAJESTY'S

The marks of the nails seemed to be recent, and further search revealed pieces of rope and timber recently cut. Bougainville estimated that the English had been there about four months before him. Actually Carteret had reached the same anchorage exactly a year previously.

On leaving the bay the routes of the two explorers diverge once more, only to meet again at Batavia. Carteret had sailed south of New Ireland. Bougainville fetched round to the north, along Dampier's track, but in the opposite direction. Like Carteret, he was anxious to reach civilisation as soon as possible, for twenty-five of his men were down with scurvy, and the remainder were exhausted and half-starved. But he did not permit their morale to suffer. "The officers set the example,

and the seamen never ceased dancing in the evening." No
"has it been necessary to double their pay"—a dig at Byron
which infuriated the translator of the French narrative.

Making his way into the Spice Islands by way of the northern
coast of New Guinea, he reached civilisation in the shape of a
Dutch factory at Boeroe in the Moluccas. He had intended, he
explained, to sail to the Philippines, but the state of his crew
compelled him to seek hospitality here. On September 28, 1768,
after a voyage lasting nearly two years, he anchored at Batavia
His description of the Parisian-like capital and its rich depend-
encies is a valuable economic document, in which he warns his
countrymen of the infiltration of British traders into these
forbidden waters.

Here he received news of his predecessors, Wallis and Carteret, though owing to their silent service tactics he got little
information about their routes. Carteret indeed had left Batavia
only twelve days before Bougainville arrived, on account of the
lengthy stay necessitated by repairs to the *Swallow*. The rest
of the story really amounts to a chase after Carteret, in order to
find out what he had discovered before Bougainville reached
home to make his own claims. At the Cape he was found to be
still a few days ahead. At Ascension they found the bottle hidden
in a rocky cleft, according to the custom of all ships returning
from the East. The paper inside informed them that the
Swallow had just sailed. On February 25 they caught up with
her. Needless to say, there is nothing in Bougainville's narrative
about the ensuing interview.

On March 16, 1769, after a voyage lasting two and a half
years with the loss of only seven men, *La Boudeuse* and *L'Étoile*
anchored in St. Malo roads. A month later Cook reached Tahiti
on his first voyage to the South Seas.

Naturally the first French circumnavigator was received with
extravagant acclamation at Paris and Versailles. But he had to
share the limelight with Aotourou—a real, live savage in their
midst! The sort of person they had been reading about for the
last twenty years. The latter's every action became the subject
of gossip in the *salons* and *cafés*. Like a sensible man, he wor

all hearts by his appreciation of French wine and food. He loved to haunt the boxes of the opera to watch the nightly spectacle of the ballet. *Mais sa grande passion,* notes a diarist, *est celle des femmes auxquelles il se livre indistinctement.* Soon he became homesick and begged to be taken back. Like the honest man he was, Bougainville kept his promise, though it cost him a third of his fortune to do so. But Aotourou died of the small-pox on the voyage south. The fate of Omai, Cook's Tahitian, who was shortly to be the season's wonder in London, was more fortunate. He did at least return to the Pacific, though it is doubtful if his glimpse of civilisation improved him in any way. A lively description of his sojourn here is given in Fanny Burney's diary. In her memoirs of her father she also tells how Cook saw a copy of Bougainville's narrative lying on Dr. Burney's table, and obligingly marked therein his own route. This copy, with Cook's pencilled route fixed with skim milk by Dr. Burney, is now one of the most precious possessions of the British Museum. Fanny's memory, however, played her false when she adds that Cook "made some curious remarks on the illiberal conduct of that circumnavigator towards himself when they met and crossed each other," for they never met; he must have been referring to the Carteret incident.

Bougainville's narrative appeared in 1771 and soon gave rise to a number of interesting speculations. Aotourou's presence had, of course, given a fillip to the gospel according to Jean Jacques. It was now generally felt that Bougainville's account of Tahiti confirmed it beyond a doubt. With complete disregard of the Fuegians and other unpleasant savages, all attention was riveted on the island where free love appeared to be the rule, and the peculiar French vice of jealousy was so noticeably absent. Philosophic minds compared the innocent caresses of the islanders with the etiquette of seduction as then practised in Europe. Voltaire smacked his lips with vicarious enjoyment and wrote a pastiche entitled *Les Oreilles du Comte de Chesterfield,* a scabrous, anti-clerical tale to which the new information about Tahitian morals gave considerable zest.

Diderot, who had helped Rousseau to compose the famous

Discourse on Inequality, produced what he called a *Supplement to
the Voyage of M. de Bougainville.* A conversation between two
Frenchmen on the moral problems raised by the circumnavigator's narrative introduces a long farewell address by an old
islander, who prophesies that the visitors will return with a
cross in one hand and a gun in the other. They will enslave
your bodies and poison your minds with unnatural notions of
right and wrong. He implores Bougainville to sail away and
leave them in peace: *l'idée du crime et le péril de la maladie sont
entrés avec toi parmi nous.* In fact Diderot even accuses the
unhappy leader of teaching the natives how to steal.

What interested him was that here in Tahiti there appeared
to be no sense of shame or sin or that sense of guilt which poisoned civilised minds. It raised the question of the origin of
modesty, nay, the whole problem of morals. Love was here
reduced to a physical appetite without its attendant spiritual
disorders. Our European laws, he argued, are thus noxious and
unnatural. *Voulez-vous savoir l'histoire abrégée de presque toute
notre misère? La voici. Il existait un homme naturel; on a
introduisit au dedans cet homme un homme artificiel, et il s'est
élevé dans la caverne une guerre civile qui dure toute la vie.*

Here was the Romantic message in a nutshell—the *Homo
Duplex* of Buffon, Rousseau, Bernardin de St. Pierre, the gospel
of Chateaubriand and Pierre Loti. Bougainville's Tahiti stimu-
lated that deep-seated desire for escape—*fuir là bas*—of which
Paul Gauguin and D. H. Lawrence have been the modern
exponents.

Since the *Supplement* was regarded as such a bombshell of
immorality, its criticisms striking at the whole edifice of western
ethics, it did not appear in print until 1796, long after its author's
death. Even then the edition was strictly limited. But Bougainville must have seen it before he died in 1811. Probably he
regarded it as just another manifestation of that revolutionary
decadence for which men like Diderot had been so largely responsible. He himself belonged to the *ancien régime*. Somehow he had survived the Terror to meet Napoleon as the young
conqueror from Italy. The latter conceived a great esteem for

this distinguished relic of a vanished age. He made him a
Count of his Empire, a Member of his Senate, and even talked
of appointing him Minister of Marine. But Bougainville was
too old for such duties. At the age of eighty-three he died, and
was buried in the Panthéon among the most honoured of the
sons of France.

Note.—Lieutenant Shortland was in command of two transports which
had carried the first batch of convicts to Botany Bay; he sailed through the
centre of the Solomons group on his way to China *via* Tinian. Two other
transports, under Captains Marshall and Gilbert, discovered the groups
named after them by following a more easterly course to Tinian. A fifth,
the *Lady Penrhyn*, suffered so severely from scurvy after leaving Australia
that she stretched across to Tahiti, discovering the Kermadec group on the
way. Her first lieutenant being recognised as one of Cook's officers, they
were royally entertained there. On her way N.W. to Tinian Penrhyn
Island was discovered. (See *Voyage of Governor Phillip to Botany Bay*,
1789.)

XI

THE END OF A DREAM

WITHIN ten years of Bougainville's return in 1769 almost every problem which had perplexed Pacific explorers for the past three centuries was solved.

He came home just in time to witness the culmination of the dispute over his beloved Falklands. The inevitable incident (which Choiseul had been anticipating for so long) occurred when the *Tamar* stopped a Spanish merchant vessel and told the Spaniards to leave the islands. After which her Captain unwisely returned home, leaving a wretched force to guard the settlement. "The most detestable place I ever was at in my life," writes the disgruntled lieutenant who was left in charge. "I have a serjeant, a drummer, and ten; my brother officer a corporal and eight, with which we are to defend a blockhouse that has not a gun in it, or a loophole cut." Of course a greatly superior Spanish force soon appeared to turn them out. Now, thought Choiseul, France will have her revenge.

But from thenceforward everything went wrong from his point of view. George III's government behaved in a most unexpected way for a British government in the eighteenth century. Lord North refused to bully Spain, or indeed to make a stand of any kind. The Whig Opposition had its chance in the great debate of November 22, 1770, but Chatham's periods thundered in vain; Burke in the Commons, and Junius in the press, continued his attack on this policy of appeasement, which was dictated solely by gross neglect of the armed forces. The King's Friends hired the redoubtable Dr. Johnson to defend them, which he did very well though he knew nothing at all about the subject. He ridiculed the idea of going to war over "the empty sound of an ancient title to a Magellanick rock . . . an island which not the southern savages have dignified with habitation . . . a nest of smugglers in peace, and in war the refuge of future Buccaniers."

In the end North did go as far as to break off diplomatic relations with Spain and another European war seemed imminent as the year drew to a close. But at that moment Choiseul himself, the prime instigator of the whole business, fell from power owing to the intrigues of Mme. Du Barry. Once he was out of the way a settlement was soon announced: the Egmont colony was to be restored, but the Spanish sovereignty was admitted. Again there was an outcry from the Whigs, but more important matters in the American colonies soon claimed their attention and the whole question was forgotten. Soon afterwards Egmont was evacuated and the islands faded from public attention until they were re-settled in 1841. The Argentine government still claims sovereignty over them.

Much the same three-cornered contest occurred at Tahiti. The British denied Bougainville's claim to the island, and the Spaniards sent three expeditions to assert theirs as soon as they heard that "*el famoso capitan Kook*" had been there. Every time Cook visited what his countrymen called King George III Island he found that rival naval officers had pulled down English symbols of authority and erected their own. Of course the old *Dolphins* who sailed with him dealt with the Spanish claims in the same way. Having found a Spanish cross inscribed "CHRISTUS VINCIT. CAROLUS III IMPERAT. 1774," they added on the back of it "GEORGIUS TERTIUS REX. ANNIS 1767, 1769, 1773, 1774 ET 1778." But the island soon ceased to be of any importance to anyone, for it was too far away for any power to make its claim effective. Before the end of the century English whalers are reported from those parts, harbingers of a new age. Ultimately it passed into French hands, and it was one of the earliest of their overseas possessions to declare for Free France in our own day.

There remained the much larger question of *Terra Australis Incognita*, as distinct from what was still called New Holland. That the prestige of the unknown continent never stood higher than when Cook sailed in the *Endeavour Bark* in July 1768, and

that this was his main objective in his first two voyages, is chiefly
due to the work of Alexander Dalrymple. History deals hardly
with the unsuccessful, and that is why Dalrymple's name is
forgotten today. But had it not been for the intransigeance of
Admiral Hawke, Dalrymple would have received the command
of the *Endeavour*, not Cook.

He had many qualifications for the task. On the recommendation of the Astronomer Royal, the Royal Society nominated him as their representative, and it was the Royal Society
who originally suggested the voyage. When in the employment
of the East India Company Dalrymple had done a good deal of
cruising and survey work in eastern waters; later he became
the first hydrographer to the Admiralty; and certainly no one
living knew more about the history of the Pacific and its
problems than he did, though he had never been there. But he
would not have been a good leader to work under. He was by
nature obstinate, opinionated and cantankerous. His eccen-
tricity, which ultimately led to his dismissal by the Admiralty,
is illustrated by the fact that though he issued thousands of
charts he never would give naval officers the ones they demanded. As an historian his books are spoiled by the fact that
they were produced with the sole aim of proving the existence
of a southern continent—"the great Passion of my life." The
result is that they are marred by distortion of fact and extreme
credulity. Above all, Dalrymple suffered from the fatal
deficiency of not being a naval officer. He refused to sail unless
he was given the command. Hawke refused to allow anyone
but a member of the service to take command of one of His
Majesty's ships, for the last time a scientist (Halley) had been
put in command the crew mutinied. Neither side would give
way, so when Admiral Sir Hugh Palliser recommended Cook,
whom he had met on the North American station, Hawke gave
the latter a commission which raised him from the rank of
Master to that of Lieutenant. It was thus with some reason that
Dalrymple spent the rest of his life grumbling about "the
influence of narrow-minded men," which had robbed him of
his great opportunity.

He was always, he claims, with his Victorian love for italics, "inflamed with the ambition to do *something* to promote the general benefit of mankind, at the same time that it should conduce to the glory and interest of my country." In a way he did, though that "something" was not the discovery of *Terra Australis*, as he had intended. While still a clerk at Madras he began his researches into the history of the Pacific. Chance, and the scholar's persistent curiosity, led him there and at home to make discoveries of first-rate importance at a time when the seamen we have been following in the last few chapters were making their voyages. His first find ("early in life" is the only date he provides) was the original of the Memorial of Dr. Arias (*c.* 1620), which alludes to the voyages of Torres and Juan Fernandez. Later, at some equally undetermined date some time after 1790, there came into his hands the original of Torres' letter of 1607, describing his Strait, which Dalrymple gave Burney to publish in 1806. It was on the strength of the Arias memorial, a thoroughly inaccurate document, that he confidently marked Torres Strait on his map which, as we shall see, helped Cook to rediscover it. Another of his finds was the Rotz map of the time of Henry VIII, which marks the northern and north-eastern coastline of Australia with such inexplicable accuracy. Indeed it was Dalrymple (rather than Flinders who popularised it) who revived the use of the name "Australia," apparently first used by a bookseller named John Dunton in 1693.[1] Thus out of the wreck of his *Terra Australis* all that he salvaged was part of the name.

His first book, which was printed at his own expense in 1767,

---

[1] Owing to war-time restrictions I have been unable to trace this allusion, which is made by Cmdr. F. J. Bayldon in R. Australian Hist. Soc. *Proceedings*, XIII, 1927. Flinders was evidently unaware of any previous use of the word, and, while suggesting it, did not use it himself: "Had I permitted myself any innovation upon the original term (*Terra Australis*), it would have been to convert it into Australia ; as being more agreeable to the ear, and an assimilation to the names of the other great portions of the earth." (*Voyage to Terra Australis*, 1814, Vol. 1, Introduction.)

As there has been persistent confusion over the date of Dalrymple's finds it may be as well to quote what he says, in view of the rarity of his books. In 1767 (*Account of the Discoveries* . . . p. xxvii) he writes : " This memorial was presented to the King of Spain by Juan Louis Arias. It is contained in a very was *An Account of the Discoveries made in the South Pacifick Ocean previous to* 1764. Though not actually published till after Cook had sailed, Dalrymple swallowed his pride and gave an advance copy of it to his friend Banks, who finally sailed as the representative of the Royal Society. On the map which it contains Dalrymple marks Torres' track from Santo through the strait between New Guinea and Australia. Cook had this map on board when he turned north-west instead of north-east, as Bougainville had done, when off the Queensland coast. None the less it is extraordinarily inaccurate for the rest of the Pacific. Dalrymple refused to believe in the existence of the Solomons, probably because his hero, Quiros, had been unable to find them. So Guadalcanal is marked as the south-east portion of New Guinea, and a few vague dots and circles represent "New Britain or the Solomon Islands." No wonder he says that Carteret expressed his surprise on being shown "that what he thought New Discoveries were well known before," and no wonder that Buâche violently attacked him for this false identification of the as yet unlocated Solomons.

The aim of this thin book, which he later withdrew from circulation, was the same as that of his larger *Historical Collection of the Several Voyages and Discoveries in the South Pacific Ocean*, which was published in 1770. It was to prove the existence of a continent which "has been seen and once visited" (presumably by Quiros). This continent had, of course, nothing to do with what we call Australia. Its western side was seen by Tasman (i.e. the western coast of New Zealand), its eastern by Fernandez, its northern by Quiros and others. In bulk it is of

curious collection of original papers, in 2 vols., taken from the archives of Spain, formerly belonging to M. Colbert's library : the papers are without order or connection; some of them MSS., some the printed memorials laid before the Councils of the Indies. Arias' memorial is in print, but without date : it appears, however, to have been presented about 1620." In 1790 (*Considerations on the Memoir of M. Buâche*) he writes : " Early in life I saw at Madras a Spanish MS. of these parts (N. Guinea, etc.) which, to the best of my recollection, contained the discoveries of Torres in 1606 on the South of New Guinea. It was amongst the papers of Mr. William Roberts, who had been a Supra Cargo to Manila and who lost his life in the siege of Madras, but on my return there in 1762 I in vain endeavoured to trace it : I am assured that the original letter of Torres dated at Manila, 12th July 1607, is still existing in Spain."

"a greater extent than the whole civilised part of Asia, from Turkey eastward to the extremity of China." The Dedication is typical, with its digs at Byron and Wallis and Bougainville, who had expressed their scepticism.

Not—to HIM—who
Discovered scarcely any thing
But
PATAGONIANS.
Not—to HIM—who
From 20° South Latitude,
Thinking it *impossible* to go
On DISCOVERY
Into 30° South.
Determined to come—HOME—round the World
Into 50° North.
Nor—to HIM—who
Infatuated with Female Blandishments,
Forgot for *what* he went *abroad*
And
Hasten'd back to amuse
The EUROPEAN WORLD
With stories of *Enchantments*
In the
NEW CYTHEREA;
But
To—THE MAN—who
Emulous of MAGALHANES
And
The HEROES of FORMER TIMES,
Undeterr'd by DIFFICULTIES,
And
Unseduc'd by PLEASURE,
Shall *persist* through *every* Obstacle,
AND
NOT by CHANCE,
But
By VIRTUE and GOOD-CONDUCT
Succeed in establishing an Intercourse with
A
SOUTHERN CONTINENT,
THIS HISTORICAL COLLECTION
OF FORMER DISCOVERIES
IN
THE SOUTH PACIFIC OCEAN
IS PRESENTED
BY
ALEXANDER DALRYMPLE.

The amount of solid research the book represents puts its author in a strong position when Cook returned from his first

voyage and Hawkesworth edited an inaccurate account of it, as
well as of the preceding English voyages. Dalrymple fell upon
this unlucky man with the acrimony of a disappointed scholar.
In his *Letter from Mr. Dalrymple to Dr. Hawkesworth occasioned by some groundless and illiberal imputations in his account
of the late Voyages to the South* (1773) he tore his rival to pieces
with such ferocity that, as we learn from Fanny Burney's early
diary, the wretched man went into a decline and shortly died.
Not only was he treated as an ignoramus and all his short-
comings mercilessly underlined, but on the strength of the
evidence in his possession Dalrymple was able to say about
Cook's discoveries, I told you so! Here were most of the
vaunted discoveries in northern Australia well known in the
sixteenth century.

Enough of these arrogant acerbities. Let us see briefly what
Cook actually did. The best way to appreciate his achievement
is to compare the map of the Pacific before his day and after. In
the north Pacific everything of importance had been discovered,
save the Sandwich group, many of the Marshall, Gilbert and
Caroline atolls, and most of the American coastline north of
California. In consequence of the voyages of a Dane in Russian
service named Vitus Behring, in 1728 and 1740, the strait which
bears his name, as also the Aleutian Islands and part of the coast
of Alaska, were discovered. Some, indeed, have claimed that a
mysterious Cossack trapper named Deshnev sailed through those
straits a century earlier; at all events, their existence was not
known publicly before the time of Behring. In the south Pacific
most of the islands between the Equator and 30° S. had been
sighted by one traveller or another, but their position, shape and
identity was not known with any exactitude. In Dalrymple's
map of what was known before 1764, the Solomons, Fiji, Samoa,
most of the New Hebrides and the Societies, are omitted;
furthermore, we have to distinguish between the real and the
imaginary—threads of coast like Tasman's west coast of New
Zealand, and hypothetical "signs of continent," "land discovered by J. Fernandez," etc. Of course, as has been seen,
much was done by the explorers of the next four years, subse-

quent to the publication of that map; but the outstanding problems of the eastern coastlines of Australia and New Zealand, and the existence of a continent lying in the region of 30° S., had yet to be solved.

It is curious that the Secret Instructions for Cook's voyages were not printed until 1928, though they are in the same bundle at the Record Office as those for Byron and Wallis. He followed them scrupulously, because, in the light of the previous experience which it has been the object of this book to describe, they showed him what to look for and where to look for it. Everyone knows that the public aim was "to observe the Passage of the planet Venus over the disk of the sun on June 3, 1769," a matter of importance both for astronomy and navigation. When Wallis returned early in 1768 his advice was taken to make the observations at Tahiti. But this scientific aim was the excuse for far-reaching colonial ambitions, and it is these which the Secret Additional Instructions describe: "Whereas there is reason to imagine that a continent or land of great extent, may be found to the southward of the tract lately made by Capt. Wallis in His Majesty's ship *Dolphin* (of which you will herewith receive a copy), or of the tract of any former navigator in pursuits of the like kind; you are therefore in pursuance of His Majesty's pleasure hereby required and directed to put to sea with the bark you command, so soon as the observation of the transit of the planet Venus shall be finished, and observe the following instructions . . . to proceed to the southward in order to make discovery of the continent above-mentioned until you arrive in the latitude of 40°, unless you sooner fall in with it; but not having discovered it in that run, you are to proceed in search of it to the westward between the latitudes before mentioned and the latitude of 35° until you discover it or fall in with the Eastern side of the land discovered by Tasman and now called New Zealand." It was left open to him to return either by the Horn or by the Cape of Good Hope. A covering letter warns senior officers not to demand sight of this most secret enclosure.

When Cook was entrusted with this task he was a man of

forty, of obscure origin and unknown to the public, though he had made a high reputation for himself in his own profession. On the other hand, Joseph Banks was a young millionaire and a well-known patron of science and the arts. He equipped the expedition so generously that a contemporary scientist writes: "No people ever went to sea better fitted out for the purpose of Natural History, nor more elegantly. They have got a fine library of Natural History: they have all sorts of machines for catching and preserving insects; all kinds of nets, trawls, drags and hooks for coral fishing; they have even a curious contrivance of a telescope, by which, put into the water, you can see the bottom at a great depth, where it is clear." Besides all this gear, Cook had the advantage of the experience of the many old *Dolphins* who sailed with him on this and subsequent voyages; Tobias Furneaux, Wallis' lieutenant, captain of the *Adventure* on the second voyage: Robert Molineaux, master of the *Endeavour*; Lieut. John Gore; Charles Clerke, who had sailed with Byron, mate in the *Endeavour*, lieutenant in the *Resolution*, and in command after Cook's death.

This was by no means the only way in which he was indebted to his predecessors. He had carefully studied conditions on board ship with a bearing on the scurvy problem, so he carried with him all the latest remedies, insisting above all on cleanliness and a balanced diet. Indeed he had to flog a couple of men at the start to force them to eat their ration of fresh meat instead of salt pork. As he wrote later, "Every innovation whatever, tho' ever so much to their advantage, is sure to meet with the highest disapprobation from seamen." The success of his precautions is well known, though his ship, like the others, suffered heavy casualties from malaria and dysentery at Batavia, and he had a good deal of trouble with scurvy on his second voyage. Like his precursors, he carried no chronometer on his first voyage; but, unlike them, his lunar observations, made with the assistance of the new *Nautical Almanac*, were astonishingly accurate. The *Endeavour Bark* was not a frigate like the *Dolphin*, nor had she a copper bottom, because Cook feared repairs might be difficult: she was a North Sea coaster, bluff in the bows, wide in the waist. She was not only of a more sea-worthy build, but she was not overmanned or overgunned as previous ships had been. Finally, he had the advantage of the very latest knowledge of what had been done in these seas before him: the books of De Brosses and Dalrymple, extracts from the logs of Tasman and Wallis (Carteret and Bougainville had not returned when he sailed).

Following his instructions, Cook sailed through the straits of Le Maire, and keeping a more direct course than that followed by the *Dolphin*, reached Tahiti on April 13, 1769, a year after Bougainville had been there. They anchored in Wallis' southern anchorage and stayed there for three months. Many old friends recognised the *Dolphins*, but O Berea seemed to have fallen from her high estate. From his own observations, and from conversations with Omai, the islander he brought back to London, Cook shared Bougainville's belief that the island was not the paradise casual observers took it for. As to love affairs, he did not share the French taste for publicity in such matters. "With respect to the amours of my people at Otaheite and other places," he informed the editor of his second voyage, "I think it will not be necessary to mention them at all."

As soon as their observations were completed, the most important part of the voyage began. Instead of continuing west, as all his precursors had done, Cook, in obedience to his instructions, struck due south to 40° 22' S. "Having not the least visible signs of land," he then worked west in broad tacks until, at the end of the year, he discovered the eastern coast of New Zealand. Banks, who had all along been sceptical about the continent, announced with satisfaction "the total destruc-tion of our aerial fabric called Continent."

Since his route was now left open to him, a conference was called at which it was decided to continue west to strike the coast of New Holland. This was done at a point south of Sydney, from which they sailed up the whole length of the eastern coast inside the Barrier Reef. This formidable obstacle being un-known to them, the *Endeavour* nearly came to grief near where the *Boudeuse* had struck a few months previously. But Bougain-

M

ville was on the outside of the Reef, Cook on the inside, and in order to extricate himself, as well as to look for the passage marked by Dalrymple, Cook continued N.N.W., whereas his predecessor had sailed N.E. After "the most dangerous navigation that ever perhaps ship was in," he found the passage in 10° 30′ S. He named it Endeavour Passage to distinguish it from Torres Strait north of Prince of Wales Island, and took possession of the whole coast he had sailed along under the name of New South Wales. He returned home via Batavia and the Cape of Good Hope.

This was the most important voyage ever made in the Pacific as much for what it did not discover as for what it did. "Although," wrote Cook, "I have failed in discovering the much talked of southern continent, which perhaps does not exist, and which I myself have much at heart, yet I am confident that no part of the failure of such discovery can be laid to my charge."

Of course that did not satisfy the continental enthusiasts. True, Quiros' land of Manicolo, south of Santo, had ceased to exist; true, there was evidently no land between Tahiti and New Zealand; but, argued men like Dalrymple, something must exist to the east of the longitude of Tahiti, viz. 150° W. in that untraversed part of the ocean where Juan Fernandez and Theodore Gerrards (of which so much had been made by the "continentalists") claimed to have seen land. Even Cook, who kept an admirably open mind about the whole business, admitted the possibility of large islands, and there were French stories about land in the south Atlantic.

So the southern continent was also the aim of the second voyage (1772-1775). Perhaps Cook had in mind Dampier's advice about crossing the South Seas in the reverse direction to that invariably followed by his predecessors, making use of the westerlies to sail from New Holland to Chile in the Horse Latitudes. Anyhow he was instructed to take the *Resolution* and *Adventure* sloops via the Cape of Good Hope as far south as lat. 54° S., in long. 11° 20′ W. (the supposed position of Bouvet's island south of Africa). Thence he was to stretch eastward and circumnavigate the globe, returning to the same spot, and "keeping in as high a latitude as you can, and prosecuting your discoveries as near to the South Pole as possible." This Cook did, reaching latitudes as high as 67° and 71° S., skirting the ice-floes of Antarctica, and twice circling the southern Pacific to give his men some relaxation from the gripping cold. By so doing he rediscovered many long-lost lands — Mendaña's Marquesas, Quiros' Santo and the New Hebrides to the south of it, Rogge-veen's Easter Island. Though he searched deliberately for them, nothing could be found of the lands seen by Fernandez and Gerrards. Returning via the Horn, he had definitely disposed of a legend which had held credence for close on two thousand years. "I have now done with the Southern Pacific Ocean and flatter myself that no one will think that I have left it unex-plored." And again, in one of his official letters: "If I have failed in discovering a continent, it is because it does not exist in a navigable sea, and not for want of looking after."

The aim of the third and last voyage (1776-1780) harks back to that of the Elizabethans: the western exit of a North-West Passage and a rediscovery of Drake's New Albion, Byron's un-fulfilled objectives. He again sailed via the Cape of Good Hope and made use of the westerlies to reach New Zealand, paid his last visit to his friends at Tahiti, and set off in search of land in 45° N. Because he followed a fresh diagonal route across the North Pacific he discovered on his way thither Hawaii and the Sandwich Islands. He made his landfall of the American con-tinent on the coast of Oregon, followed the coast up in a vain search for a way home, until he reached the Behring Strait between Asia and America. I sailed through, he writes in his last letter, "flattered with the hopes of having at last overcome all difficulties, when on the 17th of August, in lat. 70° 45′ N., long. 198° E., we were stopped by an impenetrable body of ice." He returned to Hawai where, like Magellan, he was killed covering the retreat of his men. Clerke took over the command and tried again to penetrate the Strait, but he also died before they reached home. However, Lieutenant James Burney, "my friend the Admiral" of Lamb's essays, did return to become the Pacific's first real historian.

M *

Thus in ten years, in consequence of sailing 70,000 miles between 70° N. and 71° S., throughout the whole expanse of the Pacific with the exception of the Gilberts-Solomons area, Cook had effectively exploded the ancient myth of *Terra Australis Incognita*, and had replaced it with the realities of Australia and New Zealand. How fruitful that myth was can be judged by the discoveries he and his predecessors made in their search for the substance which underlay the dream. The map of the Pacific is his monument.

It only remained to correct the details, a long and arduous task carried out chiefly by officers of the Royal Navy. How that was done, and how the ocean was invaded by a horde of whalers, missionaries, blackbirders, beachcombers, remittance men and copra merchants, does not concern us here. We have surveyed the first heroic age of European enterprise in the Pacific. After a century of commercial exploitation, which, on the whole, has done us small credit in those parts, we are fortunate to have lived to see the dawn of a second heroic age.

THE END

LIST OF BOOKS

THE following list shows the authorities for each chapter. For a general survey the most useful books have been found to be: J. C. Beaglehole, *The Exploration of the Pacific*, 1934 (the only comprehensive book on the subject); E. Heawood, *History of Geographical Discovery in the XVIIth and XVIIIth Centuries*, 1912; A. Rainaud, *Le Continent Austral*, 1893. James Burney's *Chronological History of the Discoveries in the South Sea*, 5 vols., 1803-17, remains the best collection of voyages.

For old maps see: F. C. Wieder, *Monumenta Cartographica*, 5 vols., The Hague, 1926-9; Nordenskiöld, *Facsimile Atlas*, 1889; A. L. Humphreys, *Old Decorative Maps and Charts*, 1926; E. D. Fite and A. Freeman, *A Book of Old Maps*, 1926.

CHAPTER I

Magellan, *Voyage Round the World*, ed. Lord Stanley. Hakluyt Society, 1874.

De Morga, *History of the Philippine Islands* (1609), ed. Lord Stanley. Hakluyt Society, 1868.

H. R. Wagner, *Spanish Voyages to the North West Coast of America in the XVIth century*. California Hist. Soc., 1929.

CHAPTER II

Mendaña, *The Discovery of the Solomon Islands*, ed. Lord Amherst and B. Thomson. Hakluyt Society, 2 vols., 1901.

Sarmiento, *Voyage to the Strait of Magellan*, ed. Markham. Hakluyt Society, 1894.

CHAPTER III

Quiros, *Voyages of*, ed. Markham. Hakluyt Society, 2 vols., 1904.

Drake, *The World Encompassed*, ed. Temple. 1926.

F. Riesenberg, *Cape Horn*. 1941.

J. Corbett, *Royal Geographical Journal*. June 1903.

J. Corbett, *Drake and the Tudor Navy*, Vol. I. 1899.

J. A. Williamson ed., *The Observations of Sir Richard Hawkins*. 1933.

Z. Nuttall, *New Light on Drake*. Hakluyt Society, 1914.

H. R. Wagner, *Sir Francis Drake's Voyage Round the World*. 1926.

CHAPTER IV

Quiros, *op. cit.*

H. N. Stevens, *New Light on the Discovery of Australia.* Hakluyt Society, 1929.

B. Malinowski, *The Argonauts of the Western Pacific.* 1922.

J. E. Weckler, *Polynesian Explorers of the Pacific.* Washington, 1943.

R. H. Major, *Early Voyages to Terra Australis.* Hakluyt Society, 1859.

CHAPTER V

Molyneux, *Tractatus de Globis* (1592), ed. Markham. Hakluyt Society, 1888.

Spilbergen and Schouten, *The East and West Indian Mirror*, ed. Villiers. Hakluyt Society, 1906.

De Morga, *op. cit.*

Riesenberg, *op. cit.*

Major, *op. cit.*

G. C. Henderson, *The Discoverers of the Fiji Islands.* 1933.

Blaeu map in *Royal Geographical Journal.* October 1943 (Heawood).

Tasman, *An Account of Several Late Voyages*, ed. Smith and Walford. 1694.

Tasman, *Journal*, ed. J. E. Heeres. Amsterdam, 1898.

Roggeveen, in Dalrymple (see below) and *Voyage of Gonzalez to Easter Island*, ed. B. G. Corney. Hakluyt Society, 1908.

Macmillan Brown, *The Riddle of the Pacific.*

Thevenot, *Relation de Divers Voyages Curieux.* 1664.

CHAPTER VI

Narborough in *An Account of several late Voyages.* . . . 1694.

Hacke, *Collection of Voyages.* 1699.

Esquemeling, *Buccaneers of America*, in Burney, Vol. III.

Mariner's Mirror. October 1924 and April 1927.

Dampier, *Voyages*, ed. Masefield, 2 vols. 1906.

Dampier, *New Voyage Round the World*, ed. Gray and Penzer. 1927.

Dampier, *Voyage to New Holland*, ed. J. A. Williamson. 1939.

Dampier, *Life*, by Clennell Wilkinson. 1929.

Captain Dampier, by W. H. Bonner. Stanford University Press. 1934.

Evelyn, *Diary.* August 6, 1698.

Woodes Rogers, *Cruising Voyage Round the World*, ed. G. E. Manwaring. 1928.

J. D. R. Powell, *Bristol Privateers.* 1933.

E. Cooke, *Voyage to the South Seas*. 1712.

G. Shelvocke, *A Privateer's Voyage Round the World*, ed. W. G. Perrin. 1928.

CHAPTER VII

J. Harris, *Navigantium atque Itinerantium, or A Compleat Collection of Voyages and Travels*, 2 vols. 1705. Second edition, J. Campbell, 1744-8. Third edition, 1764.

Churchill, *Collection of Voyages and Travels*, 4 vols. 1704. Vols. 5 and 6, 1732.

De La Villestraux, *Deux Corsairs Malouines*. 1929.

Frézier, *Voyage to the South Sea*, trans. 1717.

Anson, *Life*, by Barrow. 1839.

Anson, *Commodore Anson's Voyage Round the World*, by Boyle Somerville. 1934.

Scurvy, see Surgeon Rear-Admiral J. R. Muir's *Life of Cook*. 1939; and Boteler's *Discourses* (1634) in Navy Record Society. 1929.

J. Harrison, see R. T. Gould in *Mariner's Mirror*. April 1935.

De Brosses, *Histoire des Navigations aux Terres Australes*, 2 vols. 1756.

J. Callandar, *Terra Australis Cognita*, 2 vols. 1766-8.

E. W. Dahlgren, *Relations . . . entre la France et les côtes de l'océan Pacifique*. 1909.

E. W. Dahlgren, *Voyages Français* in *Nouvelles Archives des Missions Scientifiques*. 1907.

CHAPTER VIII

Byron, *Narrative of the Loss of the Wager*. 1768.

Byron, Voyage in Hawkesworth's *An Account of the Voyages. . . .* 3 vols. 1773.

Byron, Instructions printed in *Quest and Occupation of Tahiti*, Vol. II, ed. B. G. Corney. Hakluyt Society, 1913-17.

Gentleman's Magazine. May 1786.

State Trials. April 1765.

Bulkeley, *Journal*, in *An Authentic and Genuine Journal of Commodore Anson's Expedition. . . .* Anon. Second edition. 1745.

V. F. Boyson, *The Falkland Islands*. 1924.

H. Walpole, *Letters*, ed. Toynbee. Vol. VII.

CHAPTER IX

Hawkesworth, *op. cit.*
Boyson, *op. cit.*
Corney, *op. cit.* Vols. I and II.
Wallis, Instructions in P.R.O. Admiralty 2/1332, pages 145-152.

CHAPTER X

L. de Bougainville, *Voyage Round the World.* Paris, 1771. Trans. 1772.
Bougainville, *Vie*, by M. Thiéry. 1932.
J. Lefranc, *Bougainville et ses Compagnons.* 1929.
Fesche, *Journal*, ed. J. Dorsenne. 1929.
Commerson, see Corney, *op. cit.*, Vol. II.
Diderot, *Supplément au Voyage de Bougainville*, ed. G. Chinard. Baltimore, 1935.
F. Burney, *Early Diary*, 1907, and *Memoirs of Dr. Burney*, Vol. I. 1832.
P. Buâche, *Histoire de l' Académie des Sciences*, 1781 (Memoire).
C. P. Claret de Fleurieu, *Découvertes des François en* 1768 *et* 1769 *dans le sud-est de la Nouvelle Guinée.* 1790. (Trans. 1791.)

CHAPTER XI

A. Dalrymple, *An Account of the Discoveries made in the South Pacifick Ocean Previous to* 1764. Printed 1767, published 1769.
Dalrymple, *An Historical Collection of the several voyages and discoveries in the S. Pacific Ocean*, 2 vols. 1770-1.
Dalrymple, *Letter to Dr. Hawkesworth.* . . . 1773.
F. J. Bayldon, *Royal Australian Historical Society Proceedings.* 1927.
Cook, Instructions in *Naval Miscellany.* Navy Records Society, ed. W. G. Perrin. 1928.
Cook, *Life*, by A. Kitson. 1907.
Cook, *Life*, by Surg. Rear-Admiral J. R. Muir. 1939.
Cook, *Life*, by R. T. Gould. 1935.
Hansard, *Parliamentary Debates.* Nov. 22, 1770, and Jan. 25, 1771.

INDEX